BETWEEN TWO WORLDS

BETWEEN TWO WORLDS

The Commonwealth government and the removal of
Aboriginal children of part descent in the Northern Territory

Rowena MacDonald
Australian Archives

IAD PRESS
Alice Springs

First published in 1995 by
IAD Press
PO Box 2531
Alice Springs
NT 0871
Phone (08) 8951 1311
Fax (08) 8952 2527

Reprinted in 1996

National Library of Australia cataloguing-in-publication data:

MacDonald, Rowena, 1964– .
  Between two worlds: the Commonwealth government and the removal of Aboriginal children of
  part descent in the Northern Territory: an Australian Archives exhibition.

  Bibliography.
  ISBN 0 949659 87 8

  1. Photography – Australia – Exhibitions. 2. Photography, Artistic – Exhibitions. 3. Aborigines,
  Australian – Children – Exhibitions. 4. Aborigines, Australian – Government policy – History –
  Exhibitions. 5. Aborigines, Australian – Child welfare – Exhibitions. 6. Aborigines, Australian –
  Treatment – Exhibitions. I. Australian Archives. II. Title.

779.93060899915

Designed by Christine Bruderlin
Films by Lithoplatemakers, Adelaide
Printed by Prestige Litho, Adelaide
Front cover photo: Boy at the Bungalow, 1920s (Australian Archives: AA(ACT): CRSA1; 30/1542)
Back cover photos, top to bottom: Alexandria Station, Northern Territory, 1917 (National Library of
Australia, Pictorial Collection, NL27231), Domestic arts class at the Bungalow, Old Telegraph Station,
Alice Springs c.1939 (Boehm Collection, Conservation Commission of the Northern Territory,
NTHP815), School at Goulburn Island Mission, 1928 (AA(ACT): CRS A263; [43a])

Contents

Forewords

Was life for the children who were put into the government institutions at Kahlin or the Bungalow harder or easier than it was for those of us who were taken to mission homes? Physical conditions might have been easier at the church missions, but I suspect that emotionally and psychologically it may have been harsher. At least some of the kids at the Bungalow could maintain regular contact with their families.

My mother was a Yunkunytjatjara woman. My father was an Irish station manager at Granite Downs, Indulkana in South Australia. I was two years old when I was placed in the Colebrook Home for 'Half-caste' Children at Quorn. It was a church mission and my four sisters and one brother were already there. There is a photo of Colebrook on page 61 but it was taken a few years before my time there.

We were educated and well cared for. The conditions were much better at Quorn than they were for the children at the Bungalow or Kahlin. But, like these children, we were not permitted to speak our own language or retain our own names. We were given biblical names, and, like the children at the Bungalow and Kahlin, we were trained – the girls as domestic servants, the boys as stockmen.

I decided, however, that this was not for me and I struggled to pursue a career in nursing. By 1957 I was a charge sister at the Royal Adelaide Hospital, and some time later I joined the South Australian Department of Aboriginal Affairs as a nurse and welfare officer working in remote areas.

Looking at the picture of Daisy Ruddick on page 68 you may find it incredible that her brothers recognised her after sixty years. But that experience is very common among those of us who were taken away. I myself was working in Coober Pedy when two people sitting outside the supermarket spotted me and said, 'That's Lilly's daughter.' They were my uncle and auntie; they saw the family resemblance straight away and told me that my mother was living at Oodnadatta.

As soon as I could, I went to visit her. I went with my oldest sister Eileen who was already married and living in Adelaide. As soon as our mother heard about our impending visit, she waited by the roadside every day for three months until we finally turned up. In all, I was able to know my mother for ten years. I am still in touch with my Yunkunytjatjara people.

I have another family as well – the Aboriginal people who were at the Colebrook home. Some of them still live around Quorn. We have taken over the old mission. That place, after all, was the closest thing most of us had to a real home. These days it is the Colebrook Community Centre, a retirement village where we continue to look after each other.

Other Aboriginal people have not been so lucky. They have failed to find their own family or a community to which they can belong. The

Lois O'Donoghue
*Chairperson
Aboriginal and Torres Strait
Islander Commission*

scars of their shattered lives are all too visible. Others again have found their families through Link-Up, whose work, I am proud to say, the Aboriginal and Torres Strait Islander Commission helps to fund.

Between Two Worlds is an important book which every Australian should read. There is no longer any excuse for people to say that they do not know our story – now they can know our story and share in our past.

George Nichols
Director-General
Australian Archives

The exhibition Between Two Worlds helped raise community awareness of the often disastrous consequences of government policies towards Aboriginal people, in particular the removal of children of part-Aboriginal descent from their families. This book will tell the story to an even wider audience, which is a necessary step along the road to reconciliation, no matter how painful it may be.

The Australian Archives owes a great debt to Hilda Muir, Daisy Ruddick, Emily Liddle, George Bray, Alec Kruger and Herbie Laughton, who all gave freely of their time, advice and energy to share their stories. Their experiences at the institutions run by the Commonwealth in the Northern Territory mirror those of thousands of other Aboriginal people all over Australia.

Between Two Worlds is significant for the Australian Archives because the groundwork was laid in full consultation with Aboriginal people. The contacts the Archives made during the exhibition and in publishing the book have given us a better understanding of the needs and concerns of Aboriginal people. We have a clearer idea of how they and their history have been represented in the past, and the services the Archives can provide for them in the future.

Harrowing episodes in our history are etched in the memories of those affected; they are also often retained in government records. The Australian Archives' task is to ensure that the Commonwealth's memory is kept intact. Exhibitions and books like this one, drawn largely from Commonwealth records held by the Archives, ensure that our history – however grim in parts – will not be forgotten.

These records are crucially important in assisting families that were separated to be reunited. The Australian Archives is committed to giving all Australians access to records that document their history, and there are, perhaps, few records in the collection as important as those that can reunite Aboriginal families and help address past wrongs.

Just as many displaced people are now returning to their families, this story has returned to its origins in the Northern Territory for publication. The Archives is delighted that the Institute for Aboriginal Development Press in Alice Springs has published *Between Two Worlds*.

Preface

This book is based on the Australian Archives exhibition Between Two Worlds, and has its genesis in a decision by the Commonwealth government to prepare an exhibition of its records relating to Aboriginal Australians to mark the International Year of the World's Indigenous People (IYWIP) in 1993.

Rowena MacDonald
Curator

Given the vast range of Commonwealth records relating to Aboriginal people, choosing the subject of the exhibition was a formidable task. Those of us involved decided early on that this, the Archives' first major travelling exhibition, should be relevant, stimulating and challenging, and look not only at the development of Commonwealth policy, but at the impact of that policy on the daily lives of individual people.

The Commonwealth did not assume responsibility for Aboriginal affairs until 1967. Most government records relating to the daily lives of Aboriginal people before that time were generated by the states and are held in state government archives. Generally, pre-1967 records about Aboriginal Australians held in the Australian Archives relate more to Commonwealth policy development than the day-to-day administration where stories of individual people and particular events are more likely to emerge. A notable exception was the collection relating to the Northern Territory, which was directly administered by the Commonwealth from 1911 to 1978. During initial discussions, Dr Peter Read, a historian at the Australian National University, suggested that the story of the government-run 'half-caste' institutions documented in these Northern Territory records might make a stimulating theme. Throughout the development of the exhibition which saw his original idea eventually realised as Between Two Worlds, Dr Read provided guidance, encouragement and invaluable expert advice.

The need to consult with Aboriginal Australians was recognised from the inception of the project; it had also been emphasised by the Cabinet in its decision to mount such an exhibition as part of the government's IYWIP program. Once the subject of the exhibition had been determined, a reference group of Aboriginal people with some involvement in the issue of removal of children was established. The group consisted of Colleen Starkis from the Australian Archives; Brian White from the Central Australian Aboriginal Child Care Agency in Alice Springs; Barbara Cummings, president of KARU (the Aboriginal and Islander Child Care Agency in Darwin) and author of *Take this Child*; Colleen Burns, also from KARU; and Bob Randall, the Aboriginal Cultural Adviser at the Education Resource Centre, Queanbeyan and a former resident of the Bungalow. Assistance in developing particular aspects of the exhibition also came from Carol Kendall of Link-Up (NSW) Aboriginal Corporation and Gordon Briscoe, an historian and former resident of the

Bungalow. The support of the members of the reference group proved vital to the development of Between Two Worlds. They provided not only advice on all aspects of the exhibition, including its design and the terminology used in the text, but also an avenue for wider consultation about specific aspects of the exhibition's content.

Brian White, Barbara Cummings and Colleen Burns put us in touch with six former residents of government 'half-caste' homes who agreed to share their stories. It was through the words of George Bray, Alec Kruger, Herbie Laughton, Emily Liddle, Hilda Muir and Daisy Ruddick that we were able to explore the human impact of the government policy documented in the archival records. Where the documents encapsulate the views of white officialdom, the words and songs of the former residents reflect some of the responses of those affected by the official policies. Where the government letters and reports state with sometimes shocking frankness the rationalisation for the policy of removal, the oral histories reveal its shattering impact on the lives of individual Aboriginal people. Through their generous participation in the development of Between Two Worlds, George, Emily, Hilda, Alec, Herbie and Daisy gave it an added dimension which helps bring home the very real effects of past government actions on the lives of Aboriginal people today.

One of the main objectives of Between Two Worlds is to contribute to the process of reconciliation between Aboriginal and non-Aboriginal Australians. By providing an opportunity for all Australians to learn about what happened in the past, we hope to increase their understanding of the issues affecting Aboriginal Australians today. Our aim is not to condemn those responsible for the removal of Aboriginal children, but to explain how and why a practice which today seems so brutal could once have been acceptable to a majority of white Australians. We also explore the impact of removal on the lives of Aboriginal people in the Northern Territory, and consider some of their past and present responses to it. Some of those who share their stories in the exhibition fondly remember the camaraderie of life in the homes. Others, who hold much harsher memories of childhood, are still very bitter about losing contact with their families and their culture. The whole issue of the removal and institutionalisation of Aboriginal children is a very complex one with far-reaching implications. It is this complexity which we have attempted to interpret, albeit briefly, in Between Two Worlds.

While the account in chapter seven by Maise Chettle (schoolteacher at the Bungalow in the 1930s) was neither included in the text of the exhibition nor drawn from archival material, the majority of the photographs and documents presented in this book come from the Australian Archives. The process of researching this material was made considerably easier through the use of *Aboriginal and Torres Strait Islander People in*

Commonwealth Records: A Guide to Records in the Australian Archives, ACT Regional Office, compiled by Ros Fraser and published by the Australian Archives. The oral history recordings, which help bring to life the story contained in the official documents, were generously loaned by the Institute for Aboriginal Development in Alice Springs and the Oral History Unit of the Northern Territory Archives. Other organisations which provided material used in the exhibition include the Australian Institute of Aboriginal and Torres Strait Islander Studies, the Conservation Commission of the Northern Territory, the Museum of Victoria, the National Library of Australia, Mushroom Records, the Northern Territory Archives Service and the State Library of the Northern Territory.

Since Between Two Worlds began its Australia-wide tour at the Australian Museum in Sydney in October 1993, the response has been overwhelmingly positive. We hope that this book will make the contents of the exhibition accessible in a permanent form to a much wider audience, and provide readers with a deeper understanding of our past and its impact on our present.

Acknowledgements

Thank you to George Bray, Alec Kruger, Herbie Laughton, Emily Liddle, Hilda Muir and Daisy Ruddick who shared their stories.

Thanks are also due to the Aboriginal advisers for the exhibition: Colleen Burns, KARU; Gordon Briscoe, MA, Australian National University; Barbara Cummings, KARU; Carol Kendall, Link-Up (NSW); Bob Randall, Aboriginal Cultural Adviser, Educational Resource Centre, Queanbeyan; Colleen Starkis, Australian Archives; Brian White, Central Australian Aboriginal Child Care Agency.

We also wish to thank the Aboriginal and Torres Strait Islander Commission; Associate Professor Tony Austin, Northern Territory University; Australian Institute of Aboriginal and Torres Strait Islander Studies; Conservation Commission of the Northern Territory; Council for Aboriginal Reconciliation; Francis Good, Northern Territory Archives Oral History Unit; Institute for Aboriginal Development, Alice Springs; Museum of Victoria; Mushroom Records; National Film and Sound Archive; National Library of Australia; Northern Territory Archives Service; Polygram Records; State Library of the Northern Territory; David Swain.

Those involved in producing the exhibition include: Rowena MacDonald, Australian Archives (curator); Dr Peter Read, Australian National University (curatorial adviser); Hewitt Design Associates (exhibition designer); Pritchard Productions (audio-visual producer); Helen Nosworthy, National Director Public Programs, Australian Archives (exhibition manager); Gabrielle Hyslop, Australian Archives (tour manager); Kerri Ward, Australian Archives (researcher); Kate Ricketts, Australian Archives (registrar); Jutta Hosel, Kerry Allan and Jennifer Anderson, Australian Archives (reprography and conservation work); and in the production of the book: Maggie Shapley, Australian Archives (publications manager) and Tania Riviere and Andrew McKenna, Australian Archives (editors).

Special funding for the exhibition was provided by the Department of the Arts and Administrative Services. The exhibition's tour was made possible by Visions of Australia, a Federal Government Touring Program.

Introduction

Earlier this century, thousands of Aboriginal children were taken away from their families and placed in government and mission institutions. Some were never to return home. It is hard to estimate the total number of children removed in the Northern Territory. In the fifty years after 1912, probably two out of every three part-descent children spent some of their lives away from their parents as a result of the policy of removal.

In the Northern Territory many of these children were placed in two 'half-caste' institutions run by the Commonwealth government – the Bungalow in Alice Springs and the Kahlin 'Half-caste' Home in Darwin. Using a selection of the documents, photographs and oral histories presented in the exhibition Between Two Worlds, this book shows what happened to the children who were placed in these institutions. It traces their journey from one place to another and one culture to another and follows the development of the Commonwealth government policy which shaped their lives.

Australia has a long history of placing 'destitute', 'neglected' and 'delinquent' children into institutional and foster care. During this century however, governments throughout mainland Australia far more readily applied these labels to Aboriginal children, especially those of part-descent, and made it easier to remove them from their families. Furthermore, the effects on Aboriginal people were worse. Conditions in the institutions were often inferior. Children were far more likely to lose contact with their families, either as a matter of deliberate policy or because of official carelessness in recording family details. Self-identity suffered as children were taught that they were inferior.

The intentions of law-makers and administrators were usually 'humane' enough. They argued that removal of children from circumstances that offended white notions of family care gave children the chance of success in the dominant society, especially if they lost their sense of Aboriginality. Those placed in institutions were subjected to subtle and not so subtle pressure to repudiate their cultural roots. James Miller's mother recalls the staff of Cootamundra Home 'making us white – think white, look white, act white.' His Aunt Jean, indoctrinated by the fundamentalists of the United Aborigines Mission at Bomaderry, learned to fear both Aboriginals – 'knowing that they were evil, wicked' – and Jesus.[1] In the 1950s when many youngsters were placed in foster care, adopting parents – almost always non-Aboriginal – were often urged to prevent children finding out who they really were.

Powers exercised over Aboriginal people varied considerably, but commonly included an abuse of human rights. These powers were most extreme in Queensland, Western Australia and the Northern Territory where large numbers of people of full descent remained on the northern

Tony Austin

1. James Miller, *Koori: A Will to Win*, Angus & Robertson, Sydney, 1985

frontier. Here the fear of miscegenation – interbreeding between different races – was most pronounced.

In Victoria, where the proportion of part-descent people in the Aboriginal population was around 90 per cent by 1940,[2] the state government exercised least control. But this did not result in less resolve in 'saving' children. Determined for the better part of a century to force people of 'light caste' to make their way within an unsympathetic dominant society, the government drove many families off the reserves and into a precarious existence easily defined as destitute, and so inviting intervention by Child Welfare authorities. Moreover, arbitrary decisions about who was allowed to remain on stations resulted inevitably in the splitting of families. As Archie Roach has stated so powerfully in song, Victorian children like him were being sent into institutional or foster care as late as the 1950s. Only in Tasmania, with its known remnant population out of sight on Cape Barren Island, was there no specific provision for the removal of children.

Between 1911 and the Second World War Australia's estimated part-descent population grew from around 10,000 to 25,000.[3] This resulted in steadily increasing regulation of their lives, and enforcement of punitive laws including those legalising the destruction of families. The poverty caused by economic downturn, especially the 1930s depression, meant more families living in destitute circumstances, and so subject to the unwelcome attention of government and religious authorities concerned to 'rescue' the children. In Western Australia, where Aboriginal people had long made their precarious way in the dominant society's economy – overcoming discrimination and the frequent refusal of whites to allow their children to attend school – restrictions were gradually tightened. The Moola Bulla station in the Kimberley and the infamous Moore River Settlement stand out as blots on Western Australia's historical landscape. Only in 1960 did the Department of Native Welfare declare a policy of encouraging primary school age children to remain with their families rather than sending them away to school on a mission. The Commissioner of Native Welfare ceased to be the legal guardian of children only in 1963.

It has been estimated that while one in three hundred non-Aboriginal children have been removed from their parents this century in New South Wales, the numbers for Aboriginal children are one in six.[4] Another estimate for New South Wales is that perhaps 100,000 people of Aboriginal descent do not know their families or communities.[5] In that state the decision to separate 'near-white' children from their mothers dates back to 1883. Only from 1939 was a court hearing required, and then it was often a formality.

New South Wales authorities were also known to advocate the 'breeding out' of Aboriginal blood through the marriage of female inmates of the Homes to men of European descent. But only in the Northern

2. Andrew Markus, 'Under the Act' in Bill Gammage and Peter Spearritt (eds), *Australians 1938*, Fairfax, Syme and Weldon Associates, Sydney, 1987

3. Andrew Markus, 'Under the Act', 1987 and Paul Hasluck, *Shades of Darkness: Aboriginal Affairs 1925–1965*, Melbourne University Press, Melbourne, 1988

4. Stuart Rintoul, *The Wailing: A National Black Oral History*, William Heinemann Australia, Melbourne, 1993

5. Coral Edwards and Peter Read (eds), *The Lost Children*, Doubleday, Sydney, 1989

Melville Island
Roman Catholic

Kahlin 'Half-caste'
Home, Darwin
Commonwealth
government

Palm Island
State government

The Bungalow, Alice Springs
Commonwealth government

Cherbourg
State government

Warilda, Brisbane
State government

Mt Margaret
United Aborigines Mission

Colebrook
United Aborigines Mission

Kinchela Boys Home
State government

Moore River
State government

Cootamundra Girls' Home
State government

Sister Kate's, Perth
Christian independent

St Francis House,
Adelaide
Anglican

Some of the major Aboriginal settlements and institutions in which removed children grew up. (Victoria and Tasmania had no institutions specifically for Aboriginal children.)

Territory and Western Australia was this semi-official policy. In 1937 Western Australia's long-serving Chief Protector, A. O. Neville, even went so far as to applaud the existence (and compulsory institutionalisation) of children born illegitimately to white fathers and mothers of part descent – on the grounds that their complexions became progressively fairer.

More often, however, miscegenation of any kind was taboo. Prominent in Queensland's 'protective' legislation of 1897 were provisions prohibiting sexual contact between the 'races', and authorities maintained legal control over the marriage of Aboriginal people until 1965. J. W. Bleakley, Queensland's Chief Protector for four decades, saw no virtue in biological engineering through marriage, arguing as late as 1960 that 'the colour of the mind,' so much more powerful than 'the colour of the skin,' prevented people from ever losing their Aboriginality. But in spite of his belief that Aboriginal people suffered from incurably 'retarding instincts,' Bleakley at least sought with some success better conditions on the State's settlements than was common elsewhere.

The quality of education in Queensland was nevertheless low. Aboriginal children, and especially those of part descent, were looked upon throughout the country as a potential servant class on whom a sound general education was wasted. Early apprenticeship for boys, most often in unskilled trades, and equally early domestic service for girls, was taken for granted. Working conditions, even by the hard standards of the time, were usually exploitative. A fourteen-year-old girl sent from the Bungalow in Alice Springs to domestic service in rural South Australia complained to disbelieving authorities that her employer:

> hits me and Joan nearly every day, she hit me with sauce pans and anything she gets hold of. And the little boy always hits us three girls . . . and calls us black and Beast and blames us for every things if he does wrong. And she never lets us go out a tall. Every morning she wakes us up at hafe past five or quarter to four and its too early for us. We all wish we wasent hear. I rather go back than stay down hear. They all call us blacks in this house and we sleep on the floor.[6]

The break-up of families may have been practised less in South Australia where there was also less preoccupation with miscegenation. Nevertheless, the *Aborigines Act* of 1911, the *Aborigines (Training of Children) Act* of 1923, and the *State Children's Act* of 1895 gave authorities sweeping powers to commit children to an institution or to foster care. While there were many loving foster parents, foster care could simply be a means of acquiring cheap help. Lallie Lennon recalls the conditions in which she lived on a South Australian station:

> I had to work very hard. As I was too small to reach the sink I had to stand on a stool to wash up and polish the silver. Polishing the spoons hurt my hands. Because I was only little I couldn't comb my hair properly. It got knots in it, so they cut it off 'baldy' at the back and left a funny tuft on the front which they used to pull when they were telling me off. I was nine then. I had to sleep by myself in a tent or the chook house. I even had to wipe the chooks' mess off me in the morning.[7]

Institutional care and the quality of staff in South Australia as in other states varied greatly. It could be harsh, with life-long consequences. Margaret Brusnahan, raised in hard conditions in a Catholic institution, points out: 'There's a lot of pain having fingers, legs broken. But it takes a lot longer to repair spirits, minds. That takes a whole lifetime. When you're adult and you can't accept that anybody loves you, that's because some other part of you has been broken.'[8] Lewis O'Brien adds: 'Institutionalisation teaches you to suppress all emotions. You don't learn all the natural things you learn in ordinary life. In the end what it does teach you – you don't do nothing because you'll get whacked . . . When you're fostered out, you're in the same realm. You've got no rights.'[9]

Even in more caring environments, once having learned inferiority and been encouraged to reject their Aboriginal roots, most children found it

6. Tony Austin, *I Can Picture the Old Home So Clearly: The Commonwealth and 'Half-caste' Youth in the Northern Territory 1911–1939*, Aboriginal Studies Press, Canberra, 1993

7. Christobel Mattingley (ed.), *Survival in Our Own Land: 'Aboriginal' Experiences in 'South Australia' since 1836*, ALDAA/Hodder and Stoughton, Adelaide, 1988

8. ibid.

9. ibid.

hard to adjust to life outside. Some people developed a strong sense of identity with the Home in which they grew up. Doris Thompson, one of the lucky ones whose father and sister visited her regularly at the United Aborigines Mission's Colebrook Home, has fond memories of the place but nevertheless recalls, 'Once I did leave Colebrook it was really difficult to find my family and to find my own identity.'[10]

To this day many people have been unable to trace their families and communities. In the early 1980s Link-Up, an Aboriginal organisation, was set up to encourage and help people in their search. The ongoing work of Link-Up throughout Australia in reuniting people with their families and communities is related in the appendix by Carol Kendall of the Link-Up (NSW) Aboriginal Corporation.

10. ibid.

1. *Life on the fringes*

*I still remember those days. Families stuck
together, and you travelled together, you slept
together, you went to ceremonies together.*
Hilda Muir

In 1911, when the Commonwealth government took control of the
Northern Territory, home for many Aboriginals was on the fringes of
white settlements. Some Aboriginals lived in camps on cattle stations and
worked for pastoralists, while others were employed in small-scale industries like gold mining and timber cutting. A growing number of people
lived on the fringes of the Northern Territory's two towns, Alice Springs
and Darwin.

Aboriginal children of part descent were born wherever Europeans
and Aboriginals associated with each other. Sometimes the parents raised
their children together, but more often part-descent children were raised
by their Aboriginal mothers.

Many white people believed that Aboriginal mothers rejected their
part-descent children, and were ready to give them away. In fact, part-
descent children were generally loved and accepted by their people as
true Aboriginals. They shared the same kin network, ceremonial life and
traditional ties to their country as their full-descent brothers and sisters.

'Half-caste' man and woman
with their child, 1930
(Australian Archives)

Elcho Island, Northern
Territory, 1937
(Australian Archives)

Children at No. 3 Bore,
Northern Territory, c.1920
*(Ferguson Collection, National
Library of Australia)*

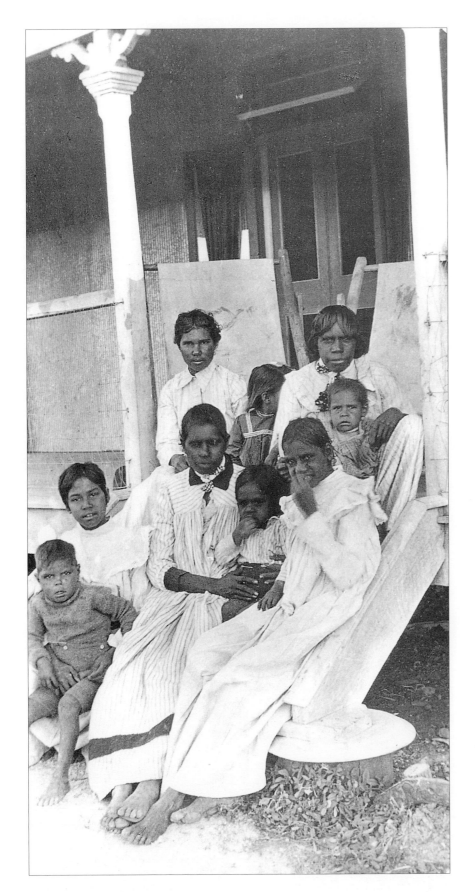

Alexandria Station, Northern
Territory, 1917
(National Library of Australia)

Mother and child, Northern
Territory, c.1928
(Australian Archives)

Aboriginal camp on Lamaru
Beach, Darwin, Northern
Territory, 1913
(Australian Archives)

Buffalo hunters, Alligator River,
Northern Territory, c.1928
(Australian Archives)

Children at Alexandria Station,
Northern Territory, c.1917
(National Library of Australia)

Bathurst Island, Northern
Territory, c.1928
(Australian Archives)

2. *Black, white and shades of grey*

The white race, in its dealings with the dark race, seems always to think in terms that involve the aboriginal as something sub-human, or, at least, outcast.
William Cooper, Australian Aborigines League, 1937

Earlier this century, many white people believed that Aboriginals were an inferior race. This belief was 'supported' by scientists who thought that each race was at a different level of development in an ongoing process of human evolution. In this 'hierarchy of races', Europeans were believed to be the most highly evolved, followed by Asians. At the bottom of the hierarchy were Aboriginals, the richness and complexity of their culture not yet recognised.

These scientific theories reinforced racist views of Aboriginal culture held by most white people. Many believed that Aboriginal ways of living were not simply different from white ways, but were inferior. They did not try to understand Aboriginal culture, and saw camp life as dirty and degrading. Aboriginal ways of rearing children seemed uncaring and Aboriginal sexual behaviour was viewed as immoral.

At this time, Aboriginals of part descent were referred to as 'half-castes'. Because they had some 'white blood' they were seen as racially superior to other Aboriginals, but still inferior to Europeans. Many believed that, given some education, 'half-castes' could be 'uplifted to the superior level of European civilisation.' The government policy of removing part-descent children from their families was based on these widely held beliefs.

In 1911 Baldwin Spencer, Professor of Biology at the University of Melbourne and respected ethnographer, was appointed as Chief Protector of Aboriginals in the Northern Territory for twelve months. Spencer's report of 1913 reflected scientific views of the day about the Aboriginal race.

(Australian Archives)

PROFESSOR BALWIN SPENCER,
Ethnologist.

(Originally published in The Bulletin, *1927)*

PRELIMINARY REPORT ON THE ABORIGINALS OF THE NORTHERN TERRITORY

BY PROFESSOR W. BALDWIN SPENCER, M.A., C.M.G., F.R.S., PROFESSOR OF BIOLOGY IN THE MELBOURNE UNIVERSITY.

HALF-CASTES.

The question of half-castes other than the children of legally married men and women is a somewhat difficult one to deal with. In the first place, the Act requires to be amended so as to include a more clear definition of a half-caste than it now does.

It is sincerely to be hoped that, as the country becomes populated, the proportionate number will become less. The first suggestion that naturally arises is their segregation into one or two special institutions designed for their training alone. I am not, however, after much consideration, inclined to favour this proposal so far as the northern part of the Territory is concerned.

The half-castes are in a most unfortunate position. There may possibly be 100-150 of them in the northern and, approximately, the same number in the southern part, where also there are quadroons who may be regarded as belonging to the white population.

I think it may be said that though the half-castes belong neither to the aboriginal nor to the whites, yet, on the whole, they have more leaning towards the former; certainly this is the case in regard to the females. One thing is certain and that is that the white population as a whole will never mix with half-castes.

It must be remembered that they are also a very mixed group. In practically all cases, the mother is a full-blooded aboriginal, the father may be a white man, a Chinese, a Japanese, a Malay or a Filipino. The mother is of very low intellectual grade, while the father most often belongs to the coarser and more unrefined members of higher races. The consequence of this is that the children of such parents are not likely to be, in most cases, of much greater intellectual calibre than the more intelligent natives, though, of course, there are exceptions to this.

The racist stereotypes shown in these cartoons from the 1920s reflect the popular white view that Aboriginals were mentally and physically inferior.
(Cross, Smith's Weekly, 1920, 1922; Glover, 'Getting near', The Bulletin, *1927; Cross cartoons courtesy of Susan Cross)*

Soap advertisement, 1920s

Squatter (facetiously): *Do you think you can get all that dirt back into the hole again, Billy?*
Billy: *Now you mention him, boss, I don't thinkit. Mine thinkit I not bin digum hole deep enough!*

GETTING NEAR.

'How do you like the new manager?'
'By cri' — you couldn't wish to loaf for a better boss.'

A selection of title pages of scientific books from 1900 to the 1930s
(National Library of Australia)

HALF-CASTES AND OTHER HYBRIDS.

There are few questions of greater difficulty and delicacy affecting the Northern Territory than the condition of half-caste children and others of mixed parentage, the offspring of that sexual relation which civilisation always and everywhere condemns, and which is particularly deplorable when it involves the mingling of the blood of white and black races. It is a frequent and, indeed, almost invariable experience that the progeny of such unions combine the defects without the virtues of the opposing stocks thus unhappily blended. The hybrids, doomed too often to a life of vagabondage, constitute a more serious problem than the blacks themselves. They are pariahs, accepted neither by white nor by black, and it is always a problem whether they have more in common with their white or with their black ancestry. What is very certain is that the people among whom they move are apt to forget the white strain in their blood, and to think only of the black, with the result that they have to carry through life the stigma of inferiority, though their intelligence is often such, as to put to shame that of their white associates. Among all who have studied them there is a feeling that they have only to be given a chance and they will respond readily enough to the discipline and conditions imposed on the white races. Where they have lapsed the fault may be less in their blood than in their environment.

This 1920s newspaper article summarises popular white views about Aboriginals of part descent.
(Australian Archives)

HOW NATIVES THINK

(LES FONCTIONS MENTALES DANS LES SOCIÉTÉS INFÉRIEURES)

BY

PROF. LUCIEN LEVY-BRUHL
OF THE SORBONNE

Authorized Translation

BY

LILIAN A. CLARE

LONDON : GEORGE ALLEN & UNWIN LTD.
RUSKIN HOUSE, 40 MUSEUM STREET, W.C.1

THE PSYCHOLOGY OF A PRIMITIVE PEOPLE

A STUDY OF THE AUSTRALIAN ABORIGINE

BY

STANLEY D. PORTEUS
PROFESSOR OF CLINICAL PSYCHOLOGY
IN THE UNIVERSITY OF HAWAII

LONDON

EDWARD ARNOLD & CO

THE RISING TIDE OF COLOR

AGAINST WHITE WORLD–SUPREMACY

BY

LOTHROP STODDARD, A.M., PH.D. (Harv.)
AUTHOR OF "THE STAKES OF THE WAR,"
"PRESENT-DAY EUROPE: ITS NATIONAL STATES OF MIND,"
"THE FRENCH REVOLUTION IN SAN DOMINGO," ETC.

WITH AN INTRODUCTION BY

MADISON GRANT
CHAIRMAN NEW YORK ZOOLOGICAL SOCIETY; TRUSTEE AMERICAN
MUSEUM OF NATURAL HISTORY; COUNCILLOR AMERICAN GEOGRAPHICAL SOCIETY,
AUTHOR OF "THE PASSING OF THE GREAT RACE"

SECOND IMPRESSION

LONDON
CHAPMAN AND HALL, LIMITED
1925

WHITHER AWAY?

A STUDY OF RACE PSYCHOLOGY AND THE FACTORS LEADING TO AUSTRALIA'S NATIONAL DECLINE

By
A PSYCHOLOGIST
and
A PHYSICIAN

Any profits accruing from the sale of this book will be devoted to the Boy Scout Movement.

AUSTRALIA
ANGUS & ROBERTSON LIMITED
89 CASTLEREAGH STREET, SYDNEY
1934

3. *The road to a civilised life*

No half-caste children should be allowed to remain in any native camp.
Baldwin Spencer, Chief Protector of Aboriginals
(1911–1912)

Aboriginal children of part descent were the object of much government attention in the Northern Territory. Officials such as Baldwin Spencer believed that because they had some 'white blood', these children could be 'civilised'. If removed from the Aboriginal camps and raised away from other Aboriginal people, they could become whites.

In 1911 Spencer chose a site for the Kahlin Compound, a camp in which all of Darwin's Aboriginals would be forced to live. When the 'Half-caste' Home opened inside the compound in 1913, it housed sixteen children. 'Before the end of 1914,' the Chief Protector forecast, 'there will be many more.'

In Alice Springs in 1913 the townsfolk erected a small iron shed, known as the Bungalow, for Topsy Smith and her part-descent children. Several years later a second shed was built to house the growing number of part-descent children who had been gathered from near Alice Springs.

The official practice of 'rescuing' part-descent children from 'the degradation of the blacks' camp' had begun. In the institutions, officials hoped, the children would be given 'a fair start on the road to a civilised life.'

Children at the Bungalow,
1920s
*(Spencer Collection, Courtesy
Museum of Victoria Council)*

RIGHT & OPPOSITE
Early government planning for
the establishment of an
institution for part-descent
children, 1911
(Australian Archives)

DEPARTMENT OF EXTERNAL AFFAIRS.

No. 11/17275.

MEMORANDUM.

  Shortly after his arrival in the Territory
Dr H. Basedow recommended the establishment of an
institution for the housing, settlement, employment
and supervision of half-castes in the Northern Territory.

  After an inspection of the land around
Darwin he suggested that blocks 391, 395 and 396 containing about 500 acres and situated about 8 or 9 miles
from Darwin be declared a reserve for aboriginals and
that permission be given to commence with the work. It
was stated that only one appointment would be needed
viz. that of a superintendent. Dr Basedow considered
the settlement ought in the course of a few years
become self supporting.

  The Acting-Administrator strongly recommended
the approval of the above suggestion.

  He was thereupon asked to state how many
people would be benefited and what kind of work
aboriginals would engage in so as to make the place
self supporting.

  A reply has now been received in which it is
stated that the number of children who would be provided for would depend upon the policy of the Government in regard to half caste children. One of the
first steps to be taken would be the gathering in of all
half castes living with aborigines. The Police could
do this work. No doubt the mothers would object but
the future of the children would he considers, out-
weigh all other considerations. Pure blooded children
might

General view of Kahlin
Aboriginal Compound,
Darwin, 1915
*(Courtesy Museum of Victoria
Council)*

11/14245

- 2 -

might also be gathered in.

The period which it would take to make the
institution self supporting would depend upon the
class of educational work undertaken, the amount of
capital expended and the quality of labour available
and employed.

He has conferred with Mr Campbell, who recently visited the Territory on behalf of the Government,
and he requests that the matter be left over until
that gentleman's return south.

At present the only places available for
neglected children are the Roman Catholic Mission at
Bathurst Island and a school conducted by Mr Barry,
a Plymouth Brother, whose work appears to be unsatisfactory as no provision is made for teaching culti-
vation or any other useful work.

23rd October, 1911.

OVER
Extracts from the
Aboriginals Ordinance 1911
which authorised the
government's removal of
Aboriginal children of
part descent
(Australian Archives)

Commonwealth of Australia Gazette.

PUBLISHED BY AUTHORITY.

[*Registered at the General Post Office, Melbourne, for transmission by post as a newspaper.*]

No. 2.]	MONDAY, 8TH JANUARY.	[1912.

THE NORTHERN TERRITORY OF AUSTRALIA.

No. 16 of 1911.

AN ORDINANCE

Relating to Aboriginals.

BE it ordained by the Governor-General of the Commonwealth of Australia, with the advice of the Federal Executive Council, in pursuance of the powers conferred by the *Northern Territory Acceptance Act* 1910 and the *Northern Territory (Administration) Act* 1910 as follows:—

1. This Ordinance may be cited as the *Aboriginals Ordinance* 1911. Short title.

2. (1.) This Ordinance shall be incorporated and read as one with the *Northern Territory Aboriginals Act* 1910, an Act of the State of South Australia in force in the Northern Territory as a law of that Territory. Incorporation.

(2.) In this Ordinance the expression "the Act" has reference to the *Northern Territory Aboriginals Act* 1910 as incorporated with this Ordinance.

C. 18459.

General power of custody and control of aboriginals vested in Chief Protector.

3. (1.) Without limiting or affecting any other powers conferred upon him by the Act, the Chief Protector shall be entitled at any time to undertake the care, custody, or control of any aboriginal or half-caste if in his opinion it is necessary or desirable in the interests of the aboriginal or half-caste for him to do so.

(2.) The powers of the Chief Protector under this section and the two next succeeding sections may be exercised whether the aboriginal or half-caste is under a contract of employment or not.

Delivery of custody or control of aboriginals or half-castes.

4. Any person having the custody or control of any aboriginal or half-caste or on whose premises any aboriginal or half-caste is living shall, on demand in writing by the Chief Protector, deliver the aboriginal or half-caste, or take all reasonable steps in his power to facilitate the delivery of the aboriginal or half-caste, into the custody of the Chief Protector or into the custody of a Protector or police officer authorized by the Chief Protector to receive the aboriginal or half-caste into his custody, and if he fails to do so shall be guilty of an offence against the Act.

Authority to police officer to take aboriginal or half-caste into his custody.

5. (1.) The Chief Protector may by writing authorize any police officer to take into his custody any aboriginal or half-caste.

(2.) The police officer so authorized may enter any premises where the aboriginal or half-caste is or is supposed to be and may take him into his custody.

(3.) A police officer who has taken any aboriginal or half-caste into his custody in pursuance of this section shall deal with the aboriginal or half-caste in accordance with the instructions of the Chief Protector.

(4.) Any person on whose premises any aboriginal or half-caste is shall, on demand by a police officer acting under this section and on production of his authority, facilitate, by all reasonable means in his power, the police officer in taking the aboriginal or half-caste into his custody.

Removal of aboriginal or half-caste from control where not properly treated.

6. (1.) Where any Protector or police officer has reason to believe that any aboriginal or half-caste is not being properly treated by any person having the custody or control of such aboriginal (whether as employer or otherwise), he may remove such aboriginal or half-caste from the custody or control of such person.

(2.) The Protector or police officer removing an aboriginal or half-caste in pursuance of this section shall forthwith give notice in writing, to the person from whose custody or control the removal is made, of the reason for the removal, and report to the Chief Protector the fact of the removal and the reasons therefor.

(3.) The Chief Protector may, if he thinks that the aboriginal or half-caste was removed for insufficient cause, direct that the aboriginal or half-caste be returned to the custody or control of the person from whose custody or control he was removed.

Unlawful entry on reserves.

7. (1.) Any person (not being an aboriginal, a Protector, a police officer, or an authorized official) who enters or remains on a reserve for aboriginals shall be guilty of an

The Bungalow, Alice Springs,
1921
(Australian Archives)

Children at Kahlin Compound,
Darwin, 1915
*(Courtesy Museum of Victoria
Council)*

Children at Kahlin 'Half-caste'
Home, Darwin, 1920s
(Courtesy Daisy Ruddick)

4. *The last goodbye*

They just come down and say, 'We taking these kids.' They just take you out of your mother's arms. That's what they done to me. I was still at my mother's breast when they took me.
Alec Kruger

Most Aboriginal communities across the Northern Territory knew the pain of separation when their children of part descent were taken away.

It was usually the local policeman, acting in the role of Aboriginal Protector, who would come to remove the children from their families. In one journey he might visit several pastoral stations or Aboriginal camps, rounding up as many light-skinned children as he could find to be brought in to Alice Springs or Darwin. He would usually try to convince the child's mother to hand over her child. If she refused, the child might be taken by force.

Parents occasionally placed their children in the homes by choice while they went to find work out bush. Sometimes the mother would go with her children to the home, where she might work without pay at the Bungalow as a domestic, or live on the other side of the fence in the Kahlin Compound. Some mothers never saw their children again.

'Half-caste' mother and child
(Australian Archives)

Alec Kruger

I was born at Katherine in 1924. I was taken away from my mother when I was three and a half years old. With a few others we were taken to Darwin to a place called Kahlin Compound and stayed there for two years. The place was real rough out there with hardly any food to eat and that. We were treated very bad there.

Group of prisoners, witnesses, interpreters and part-descent children being taken by police to Alice Springs in the 1930s. The children were bound for the Bungalow.
(Northern Territory Archives Service)

Northern Territory police
officers, 1938
(Australian Archives)

This photograph was taken by
Northern Territory police officer Bill McKinnon. His original
caption reads: 'In 1932 I had
the job of taking this half-caste
child from its parents and taking her to Alice Springs
Government Half-caste
Institution. Such jobs were
most unpleasant and even dangerous.' *(Northern Territory
Archives Service)*

George Bray

*My name is George Ernest
Bray. I was born in June the
second 1927 at a place called
Stone Well, which is out at Mt
Riddock Station. And I grew
up there till I was about nine
and a half years old and then I
was brought into the Bungalow
to attend school. The police
came out there and said it was
government policy that all
part-Aborigine kids must have
an education.*
*Dad didn't like it very much,
and neither did Mum. It was
the first time I'd been away
from home – or any of us kids
been away from the parents. I
was very disturbed, broken-
hearted, crying most of the
time, and I didn't like it one bit.*

Hilda Muir

*Families stuck together, and
you travelled together, you
slept together, you went to
ceremonies together. All those
are still clear in my mind, you
know, the days where I
roamed gathering yams and
berries, and goannas, bandi-
coot. All those are very clear. I
used to love roaming the
country after the bushfire. I
used to love the smell after the
bushfire.*
*That was the early years,
when the government decided
to pick up children from
camps and environments, and
bring them into civilisation.*

OVER
The Borroloola Police Journal
of 1928 records Hilda Muir's
removal to Kahlin 'Half-caste'
Home in Darwin.
*(Northern Territory Archives
Service)*

Wednesday 11th Continued

W.E. Harney arrived from Survey Camp at the
Island, brought Surveyor Smith & Lindsay. & Survey
Hands. Bryant & Suckling & McGrath, & later the
Survey Crowd left per Motor Lorry enroute Newcastle
Waters

H. Condon arrived from McArthur Station

P.Hs Conway ⁽⁺⁾ Calvert ⁽⁺⁾ Confusion " Concussion "⁽⁺⁾ Verbena ⁽⁺⁾

Thursday 12th

Mc. Bragland Town and Station duty.

McMorey & Tracker Harry absent on Patrol

Tracker Fred attending P.Hs Witness & Prisoners

Prisoners in Gaol Tommy Dodd & Gilbry.

Sick Abo's being treated Clara & Minnie

15 meals. Witness's Ida - Peter Melba - Pharis & Melba. 15 meals

Half Caste Hilda Nama brought to Station by

2 Meals. her mother 2 meals Supplied

P.Hs Blanco " Blittner " Blake " Brocks " Boss " New Shoes.

Friday 13th.

Mc. Bragland Town & Station duty

Tracker Fred attending P.Hs Witness's & Prisoners.

Prisoners in Gaol. Tommy, Dodd & Gilbry.

Sick Abo's being treated Clara & Minnie

15 meals. Witness's Ida - Peter - Melba - Pharis & Melba at Station 18 meals.

3 meals. Half Caste Hilda Nama 3 meals.

P.Hs Shod. Donny ⁽⁺⁾ Cora ⁽⁺⁾ & Bounce ⁽⁺⁾ New Shoes.

Issued Alic Licence to J. O'Keeffe No. 157.

At 5pm Mc. Morey. Tracker Harry & Quadroon Girl

3 meals Sarah ³ᵐᵉᵃˡˢ returned from McArthur & P.Hs report following

Duties performed & Distances travelled

Tuesday 10th To Eurn Creek 26 miles

Wednesday 11th To McArthur Station & then on to Lila Lagoon 30 miles

Thursday 12 To McArthur Station & picked up Quadroon girl Sarah
& then on to Eurn Creek 1 meal.

Sunday 15th 1928.

M.C. Brudgland & Morey, Town & Station duty.

Trackers Harry, & Fred attending P.H's.

Prisoner in Gaol Tommy Dodd.

3 meals   Prisoner Gilby. 3 meals.

6. meals.   Half Caste Hilda Hanna & Quadroon Sarah 6 meals.

Witness's Ida - Melba - Phario - Peter & Melba at Station

15 meals.   15 meals.

Sick Abo's being treated Clara & Minnie

M.C. Morey took Photo of the late Constable Lyon's

grave

M.C. Brudgland preparing to leave tomorrow.

Monday 16th 1928.

M.C. Brudgland & Morey Town & Station duty

Trackers Harry & Fred attending P.H's

Prisoner in Gaol Tommy Dodd.

Prisoner Gilby, one meal

2 meals

5 meals.

P.C. Brudgland   Half Caste Hilda Hanna & Quadroon Sarah 2 meals

Left.   Witness's Ida Melba. Phario - Peter & Melba 5 meals

At 10 am. M.C. Brudgland Tracker Fred P.H's

Bounce - Blanco - Butterfly, Boy Brooks & Butcher

Bellman - Blunt - Blake - Blither - Barnett

Boss - Conway - Cora - Concussion - Calvert -

Confusion - Dinny & Verbena with Prisoners

Gilby & Witness's Ida - Melba - Phario - Peter - Melba

Sick Abo's Clara & Minnie Half Caste Hilda Hanna

& Quadroon Sarah. left enroute Kialaauka

P.H'l   M.C. took following Mail for Head Office

~~following mail posted~~

Journal from Feb. 6th to April 1st 1928

Re Dingo Notice J. Webb. Wearyan Dawar

Quarterly Abo. Ammunition and Patrol

5. *Breed him white*

When Dr Cook was there he never wanted us to mix with the full-blooded Aboriginals. He kept us away . . . he wanted us to marry into white and get rid of our own Aboriginality.
Daisy Ruddick on Kahlin

By the late 1920s, the government's policy of removal had become more strict and purposeful. Under the direction of Dr Cecil Cook, the Chief Protector of Aboriginals from 1927 to 1939, policemen gathered up children 'from Port Keats to the Petermann Ranges' for placement in the Bungalow, Kahlin or the church missions.

The policy became more strict because the white people of the Territory feared that they would be outnumbered by the growing part-descent population. They believed that part-descent children might 'revert to savagery' if left in the Aboriginal camps or 'drift to become a menace to society.'

Dr Cook believed that the best way to prevent such problems was to eventually eradicate the part-descent population. He thought this could be achieved by removing part-descent girls from Aboriginal camps and educating them to a standard which would allow them to marry white men. The children of these marriages would also marry whites and, over several generations, all 'Aboriginal blood' would eventually be 'bred out'.

Kahlin 'Half-caste' Home,
Darwin, 1928
(Australian Archives)

J. W. Bleakley, Queensland's
Chief Protector of Aboriginals
and Dr Cecil Cook, the
Northern Territory's Chief
Protector, 1928
(Australian Archives)

Two girls at the Bungalow,
1920s *(Australian Archives)*

OVER
J. W. Bleakley, Queensland's
Chief Protector of Aboriginals,
was appointed to investigate
the condition of Aboriginals
and 'half-castes' in the
Northern Territory. In his 1928
report he recommended that
'half-castes' continue to be
removed from Aboriginal
camps for placement in institutions. *(Australian Archives)*

1929.

THE PARLIAMENT OF THE COMMONWEALTH OF AUSTRALIA.

THE ABORIGINALS AND HALF-CASTES

OF

CENTRAL AUSTRALIA AND NORTH AUSTRALIA.

REPORT

BY

J. W. BLEAKLEY,

CHIEF PROTECTOR OF ABORIGINALS, QUEENSLAND.

1928.

Presented by Command ; ordered to be printed, 8th February, 1929.

[*Cost of Paper* :—Preparation not given ; 900 copies ; approximate cost of printing and publishing, £145.]

Printed and Published for the GOVERNMENT of the COMMONWEALTH of AUSTRALIA by H. J. GREEN, Government Printer for the State of Victoria.

No. 21.—F.1882.—PRICE 3s. 6D.

Policy necessary.—A definite policy, framed upon understanding of the peculiar position and characteristics of the half-castes, and aiming at what is likely to be best for their future happiness and usefulness, should be formulated. Rescued from the camps and given opportunity for education and vocational training, they can be made an asset to the Territory. Left in their present position, they are more likely to be a menace, and, with what is an even more deplorable result, the increase of the quadroon element. All half-castes of illegitimate birth, whether male or female, should be rescued from the camps, whether station or bush, and placed in institutions for care and training. Even where these children are acknowledged and being maintained by the putative fathers, their admission to an approved institution for education should be insisted upon. The education should be simple in nature, but aimed at making them intelligent workmen and fitting them to protect themselves in business dealings. The vocational training for the boys should be in the trades already mentioned, as necessary for skilled station work, and, for the girls, the domestic arts to make them not only good servants but capable housewives. On completion of their training, those recommended as suitable for outside employment should be transferred to the control of the Chief Protector, who would satisfactorily place them and exercise supervision as long as might be necessary.

Departmental Control.—The provision in the present ordinances for departmental control of all half-castes, and even quadroons, where necessary, is a wise one, for these people, especially when uneducated, are generally as much in need of protection as the full blood, in fact are frequently more exposed to temptation and abuse.

Measures for the future of Half-castes.—Opinions vary as to what measure should be adopted for the future of the half-caste, but most people fail to make any distinction between the different breeds. The half-caste with 50 per cent. or more aboriginal blood or of alien blood cannot be fairly classed with the quadroon or octoroon. The latter should be separately considered.

Two suggestions have been put forward, viz.:—

(a) Complete separation of the half-caste from the aboriginals, with a view to their absorption by the white race ;

(b) Complete segregation from both blacks and whites in colonies of their own and to marry amongst themselves.

Past experience, however, has shown that the half-caste, with few exceptions, does not want to be separated from the blacks, in fact is happier amongst his mother's people. He is not wanted by the whites, nor does he want to be pushed into a society where he is always an outcast. He should certainly be rescued from the degradation of the camps and given the benefit of education and training, but will be happier if raised to this civilization in company with the young aboriginals of his own generation.

Marriage of Half-castes and Full Bloods.—Like every one else, the half-caste prefers to marry where fancy dictates, and where there is freedom of choice it is frequently made from amongst the full bloods. Provided the latter have been lifted to an equally civilized plane, these unions are for the benefit of both sides.

Object of training.—The object of the training of the young half-caste should be to fit him to fill a useful place in the development of the Territory, for the industries of the country can readily absorb all trained labour, either black or brown. As the latter's associates will always be his mother's race, there seems little sense in trying to create a gulf between them.

Exemption of superior type.—Half-castes showing the desire and capacity for raising themselves can be treated as special cases and given an opportunity to do so. As the superior type would probably be less than 10 per cent, to legislate for the whole on that small minority would only be courting certain failure.

Marriage of half-castes to Europeans.—Some of the superior half-caste or quadroons may help to solve the sex question, by marrying men in the outback not able to get wives of their own colour. Though one such marriage of a girl from Groote Eylandt appears to have been successful, most of the few unions of this sort observed did not seem to be very happy ones. The best type of white man is not anxious to outcast himself in this way, preferring, if he must, to satisfy his lust with casual lubras until able to return to white society.

Suitable missions for half-castes.—The two missions, Bathurst Island and Goulburn Island, could receive children from the western and northern areas of North Australia, Hermannsburg Mission those collected in Central Australia, and Groote Eylandt those from the Gulf side, the destination of the children, as rescued, being decided by the Administrator.

The Bungalow, Alice Springs,
1928
(Australian Archives)

Letter from Dr Cecil Cook
regarding his plan to eventually
eliminate the part-descent
population by 'breeding out the
colour', 1933
(Australian Archives)

OPPOSITE PAGE
This newspaper article reflects
white fears of the 1930s about
the growing part-descent
population in the north.
(Australian Archives)

COMMONWEALTH OF AUSTRALIA.

NORTHERN TERRITORY MEDICAL SERVICE,

No.

DARWIN, 7th. February 1933.

His Honour,
    The Administrator of the
        Northern Territory,
        D A R W I N.

PERMISSION TO MARRY ABORIGINALS.

With further reference to previous memoranda in
which I have called attention to the very grave problem which
has been developing in Northern Australia owing to the inter-
marriage of alien coloured races with aboriginals and half-
castes, it is strongly recommended that the Commonwealth take
action to have the States, particularly Queensland and Western
Australia, adopt a policy uniform with that of the Commonwealth.

For years it seems that Protectors of Aboriginals
have regarded it as undesirable that a half-caste or quarter-
caste aboriginal should be mated with a white. On the other
hand mating with Japanese, South-Sea Islanders, Chinese and
hybrid coloured aliens has been regarded as a very desirable
solution to what was regarded as the marriage problem of
coloured girls some of whom had over seventy-five per cent
white blood. The result has been the accumulation of a
hybrid coloured population of very low order. I am unable
to speak for Western Australia and Queensland but these coloured
individuals constitute a perennial economic and social problem
in the Northern Territory and their multiplication throughout
the north of the continent is likely to be attended by very
grave consequences to Australia as a nation.

In the Territory the mating of aboriginals with
any person other than an aboriginal is prohibited. The mating
of coloured aliens with any female of part aboriginal blood is
also prohibited. Every endeavour is being made to breed out the
colour by elevating female half-castes to white standard with a
view to their absorption by mating into the white population.
The adoption of a similar policy throughout the Commonwealth
is, in my opinion, a matter of vital importance.

(C.E. Cook).
Chief Protector of Aboriginals.

HALF CASTE — AUSTRALIA'S TRAGEDY...

Sunday 2/4/33

Half-caste girl and her quadroon baby at Alice Springs.

By ERNESTINE HILL

THE overwhelming problem of the north-west and north of Australia at the present time is the steadily increasing propagation of a half-breed race. The inevitable early history of every country where the white has made conquest of the black, it has been solved in many other instances by the swiftly-following influx of great populations, or by those countries rapidly taking their places as cosmopolitan stations upon the highways of international trade. In isolated North Australia, in 100 years, there has been no such redemption, nor, at present showing, is it probable.

In the last ten or 15 years the half-caste population of the Northern Territory has practically trebled itself. At Darwin and Broome and Alice Springs the half-castes are so numerous as to excite no comment, and scattered about on the camps and stations of a million square miles, their parentage in many instances unknown, have become a responsibility of which the north, under the best and brightest circumstances, could not now be freed in a century.

In nearly three years' experience in the far outback of Australia, chary at first of a tremendous social problem where only fools rush in with superficial judgments, I have met and observed many half-castes, to find them mostly cleanly, helpful and worthy, only too anxious to realise the best of their white derivation, but, except in very isolated instances, prevented from doing so by the mighty marshalled forces of heredity and environment, that make playthings of us all.

Travelling with the pack-teams in the wilderness, born stockmen and excellent riders, forever anonymously, and with no possible reward save the necessities of daily life, they are playing a very considerable part in the colonisation of a country actually more closely theirs than our own.

White in all save color, an outstanding few have won through. One of these is Bennie Hughes, of Cooper's Creek, station overseer and master drover, well-known from Innamincka to Oodnadatta as a reliable cattleman, a shrewd business head and a generous employer of white men. A second is Harry Stott, for many years manager of Nutwood Downs on the Roper; a third, Baden Bloomfield, of Alice

UNRECOGNISED by his father and unwanted by his mother, yet a little human boy to whom the morning life is just as fresh and sweet as to any other, he is the sad, futureless figure of the north—half-caste.

Child of a tragedy far too deep for glib preaching, half-way between the stone age and the twentieth century, his limited intellect and the dominant primitive instincts of his mother's race allow him to go thus far and no further. Lost to him are the corroborees, the happy, careless wandering of an unclad sylvan people who pick up their food where they find it, and sleep beneath the trees.

He thinks—and is therefore accursed.

Springs, perhaps the finest horseman of the Centre, who invariably shames metropolitan jockeys at the annual races, and is accepted everywhere by the white people for his sterling character and intelligence, as friend and equal.

Yet another, a charming quadroon girl educated in the Darwin Convent, is an accomplished musician, and an efficient clerk of some years' standing in a Government department, one of the most graceful and attractive feminine personalities of Darwin. At 23, engaged to be married to a white pearler, this girl is a striking example of the apparently complete triumph of environment over heredity in two generations.

As saddlers, stockmen, teamsters, sailormen, blacksmiths and overseers of outcamps and droving plants, well-trained half-caste boys can always be assured of a good living where they are known. The girls make excellent domestic helps and first-class needlewomen. In all instances, teachers who have dealt with them in the motley schools of outback have learned to appreciate the quick response of these eager, sensitive little souls to kindliness, and to deplore the fact that life has so little to give them.

For in all cases other than those of unremitting vigilance and personal direction, education proves utterly worthless, and early adolescence finds a practically complete and inevitable reversion to the black.

One of the most poignant of innumerable cases is that of a half-caste of Darwin whose life is a psychological treatise in itself. His father, who still lives, was one of the first buffalo-shooters to land on Melville Island, 40 years ago. On two occasions this man was saved from death at the hands of hostile natives by the intervention and devotion of a young lubra. In his gratitude and honorable affection he married her. The eldest son, a normal, intelligent boy, was sent to one of the principal colleges of Adelaide to be educated, and returned at the age of 18 a splendid physical specimen, sports captain of his school, with innumerable silver cups and trophies for distinction in games. He was given a responsible position in Vestey's meatworks when it was operating, and became the captain of the first football team in Darwin.

To-day, in the early thirties, on the banks of a river on the rim of Arnheim Land, with a camp of uncivilised blacks his only associates, this boy is maintaining himself by means of a crude sawmill with which he cuts cypress pine. His defence, in answer to the reproach of a white resident, devoid of all bitterness yet epic in its tragedy, is worthy of a philosopher.

"I could never have hoped to marry a white girl," he said quietly. "Had I married a half-caste, my children would be as unhappy as I have been. I prefer to go back to my mother's people."

In the early days the half-castes were often acknowledged, reared and loved by their pioneer fathers, for the sheer humaneness of their association in a cruelly lonely country. In later years, even to-day, very largely the children of derelict wanderers, they have been left haphazard in the blacks' camps, to live, or more happily sometimes, to die.

The attitude of the lubra to these children is problematic. In some instances they treasure the "little yella-fella," as they call him, with the utmost maternal love, trekking hundreds of barren miles with the child in their arms to avoid its being taken, and weeping bitterly at giving it up. In others they callously leave it at birth upon the track, or perhaps bury it in a snake-hole or rabbit-burrow. As this uncertain fate is shared by the full-blooded black babies, it can scarcely be ascribed to a racial prejudice.

So grave has the problem become in recent years, with 800 half-castes now in the Territory as against a diminishing population of between two and three thousand whites, that the Commonwealth Government, in prudence and humanity, has been forced to decisive action. During the last seven years the rising generation has been gathered in by the police patrols, from all the camps and stations from Port Keats to the Petermann Ranges, to be housed and educated in institutions.

For the first time in the history of the Territory an adequate home has been established, at the expense of thousands of pounds, three miles from Alice Springs in the Centre, to which children from a thousand miles' radius are to be removed. Under the best conditions, they are to be given every opportunity to outgrow their heredity. They will be encouraged to live white, think white, and to marry, if possible, into the white race, or failing that with each other.

With the transport of all boys from North Australian insti-

IS there a throw-back to the Australian black? Dr. Cecil Evelyn Cook, anthropologist, biologist, bacteriologist, Chief Medical Officer and Chief Protector of Aborigines in North Australia, after seven years' closest observance of the half-castes, quadroons and octoroons of the north, says no. "The Mendelian theory does not apply," said Dr. Cook. "There is no atavistic tendency as in the case of the Asiatic and the negro. Generally by the fifth and invariably by the sixth generation, all native characteristics of the Australian aborigine are eradicated. The problem of our half-castes will quickly be eliminated by the complete disappearance of the black race, and the swift submergence of their progeny in the white." Following a definite policy of concentrating the half-caste in the towns, breeding him—or rather her—with the whites to every possible extent, and where that is not possible establishing colonies of double half-castes rather than let them revert to the black, Dr. Cook has aroused much contention in the Far North.

On account of the lamentable scarcity of white women, settlers, fettlers, and bushmen of the Territory are encouraged to marry half-caste and quadroon women. They are allowed, under strictest supervision, to select a girl who appeals to them from the training-schools of the Darwin Compound and the mission stations, and, provided that they are in a position adequately to maintain her and her children, to marry her.

These marriages are taking place at the rate of three or four a year. Some of them have been happy and satisfactory. Some have not.

"The Australian native is the most easily assimilated race on earth, physically and mentally," asserts Dr. Cook. "A blending with the Asiatic, though tending to increased virility, is not desirable. The quickest way out is to breed him white."

The Territory generally is not in accord with him. Even old bushmen, who are themselves the fathers of half-castes, and have studied the question all their lives, firmly believe that it cannot be done.

Dr. Cook is about to prove it.

The new half-caste compound where the old telegraph station was at Alice Springs.

Oval: A typical half-caste boy with native lilies.

tutions, and a scouring of the Territory by camel and pack-horse police patrols, it is intended that 150 children shall be in residence there by the end of the year, leaving a residue of some 45 girls under the age of 14 at the Compound Home at Darwin.

Humane, parental, and exceedingly optimistic, this scheme frankly appals many residents of the Territory, who openly state that it is not only Quixotic and a moral cruelty to the half-castes themselves to sever them from their own country and their own people, where their man-power can be of infinite use, but the deliberate concentration of a large colored element in the settlements and railway thoroughfares that can only result in untold chaos and disaster.

A vitally interesting national experiment, it will require the passing of at least 20 years to write the end of the story.

Typical group of halfcaste children the care of the Government Officers.

Another group of half-caste children at Alice Springs.

6. *Life in the homes*

It wasn't fit for a dog to live in.
Emily Liddle on the Bungalow at Jay Creek

As more and more children were removed from their families in the 1920s and 1930s, both the Bungalow and the Kahlin 'Half-caste' Home became overcrowded. Little was done by the government to improve poor living conditions. In 1921, fifty-two part-descent children were housed in the Bungalow's three iron sheds behind the back fence of the Stuart Arms Hotel. The permanent white population of Alice Springs at this time was only thirty.

Following protests from outraged visitors, the Bungalow and its inmates were moved in 1928 to a temporary site at Jay Creek, 40 kilometres from Alice Springs. Here, living conditions were not much better, despite the efforts of the Matron, Ida Standley.

In 1932 the Old Telegraph Station, 5 kilometres from Alice Springs, became the new site for the home and its sixty inmates. By 1935, 130 part-descent children lived there. Conditions deteriorated so much that by 1939 one official was moved to write, 'I went very carefully through this building this week and to use entirely unofficial language, the whole place stinks and is in an exceedingly bad condition.'

Darwin's 'half-caste' home was originally located within the Kahlin Aboriginal Compound. Due to growing concern about the 'degenerative influence' this environment might have on the children, a house just outside the compound was taken over in 1924. By 1928, seventy-six inmates, including nine part-descent adults, lived in 'a house large enough for only one family.' Living conditions here were little better than at the Bungalow.

This photograph was taken by Dr W. D. Walker who visited the Bungalow at Alice Springs in 1928. His original caption reads: 'Half caste children at the Alice Springs Bungalow having their "daily tub". Were it not for the kindly ministrations of Mrs Standley . . . the present cleanly and happy state of these children could not be maintained under the existing extremely unsatisfactory conditions.'
(Australian Archives)

Meal time at the Kahlin 'Half-caste' Home, Darwin, 1930s
(E. H. Wilson, courtesy AIATSIS pictorial collection)

Meal time at the Bungalow, 1928
(Australian Archives)

Emily Liddle

It was just concrete floor, no beds, one big shed was built there, and a little bit of kitchen on one side, where the girls used to do the baking and that. They had to do baking and all in the two stoves they had.

We used to [laughs] get no mattress; only blankets to sleep on. We used to put all the stools up and we used to sleep on those concrete floors. Two or three girls would get together – no pillows, the concrete floor we slept on, you wouldn't even let your dog sleep on it, it was so rough. Winter time it was freezing.

WEEKLY DIET LIST FOR INMATES OF THE HALFCASTE HOME .

DINNERS.

Sunday - Corned beef, onions, potatoes, cabbage and turnips
(when available)
Plum pudding and custard.

Monday - Fried Steak and onions (older girls) Potatoes
Irish Stew (Younger girls)   "

Rice pudding.

Tuesday - Curry and rice (older girls) Potatoes.
Stew (younger girls)

Bread pudding.

Wednesday - Irish Stew.   Custard and apples.

Thursday - Roast beef - onions and potatoes

Rice Pudding.

Friday - Curry and Rice (older girls) Potatoes
Irish Stew (younger girls)   "

Bread Pudding.

Saturday - Roast Beef onions, potatoes.

Rice Pudding.

(Note: Marmite is used in all stews)

BREAKFAST   Every day - Rice, milk, bread (syrup, jam or dripping
Tea.

Morning and afternoon lunches - Bread - cocoa or milk (young girls)

TEA

Week days   Bread (jam or syrup)
Fish (when available)
Fruit 4 meals per month
Onion and tomato salad - (once a week)

Sunday.   Bread (Jam or syrup) Onion and tomato salad.

Custard and prunes.

Alec Kruger

The food at the Bungalow was real awful. For a morning meal, you just got porridge with a little sugar on it, that's all you got. Then for dinner time, and at midday meal, it was stew mostly, supposed to be vegetable, what you grew you know. You might have a few pieces of meat in it and then like, even at tea time, it was just only a slice of bread and treacle. And you couldn't ask for more. We used to go hungry all the time, we used to go hungry at night you know, cry with hunger at night you know, we couldn't sleep. That's cruel that.

A lot of people don't believe that. And you know the punishment we used to go through, say if we was hungry – and we had a big garden, we used to grow them vegies – but yet we couldn't pull a carrot up and eat a carrot: if you were caught, you was flogged. See and another thing, if you were caught pinching them another punishment was – you know those fence posts? – they used to make you stand on one of those with just a pair of trousers on, a pair of shorts, cold on winters night.

There was a town dump about five or six mile away up town, we used to go and scrounge in the dump, like getting food you know, from the dump.

OPPOSITE PAGE
This weekly diet list for the Kahlin 'Half-caste' Home was the official ideal. Few former residents recall regularly eating roast beef or fried steak. *(Australian Archives)*

Article from the Sydney *Bulletin* condemning poor conditions at the Bungalow, Jay Creek, 1929
(Australian Archives)

Original caption:

The rector of Port Lincoln (S.A.) just back from a visit to Central Australia, has recited a nasty oft-told tale: "The accommodation provided for half-caste children at Jay's Creek near Alice Springs is appalling. About 50 boys and girls, of ages ranging from 1 to 16, are herded together in one room about 48ft by 24ft. No attempt is made to separate the sexes." Again and again it has been promised that this scandal would be ended; and apparently it hasn't been ended. Above are photographs taken a few months ago at Alice Springs by Dr. W. D. Walker. (Left) A whole family sleeps on one blanket. (Middle) Males and females sleep alongside one another. (Right) The ages of these people range from newly-born to 25 years. "Babies," Dr. Walker writes, "are born in the open amongst this tangled mass of half-white-half-black humanity without any privacy whatever."

A SQUALID HORROR

—◆—

THE ALICE SPRINGS BUNGALOW

CHILDREN HERDE D LIKE SWINE

(Written for "The Daily Mail," by M. H. Ellis.)

One hesitates generally to say anything is a scandal. There is no need for hesitation in saying it about the half-caste children's "bungalow" at Alice Springs, because that is an institution which must make everyone who sees it burn with indignation. It is more than a scandal. It is a horror.

The best that can be said of it is that it is reasonably clean, but that is the fault of its mistress and not of the Commonwealth Government and of those Federal Ministers and members who let it remain as a blot on Australia.

The bungalow stands in the very middle of the town, opposite the police station, and next door to hotel. It was built to house a woman and her ten children. It has lived to house 60 children—half-caste boys and girls, ranging from babyhood to 16 years of age, and often as white as any other Australian.

There are two buildings. One so far as I could measure it by stepping the distance, is 70 feet by about 18. Thirty girls approximately inhabit this. The second is about 24 by 15 feet. This houses the boys—30 and often more of them.

IRON KENNELS.

The material of the buildings is galvanised iron. The method by which they have been built is this: Upon a rectangular frame sheets of iron were nailed. A few sheets were left out to allow a door to be inserted on each of the long sides of the building. On each side of the door a sheet was left out to make a window. There is no glass in the windows; they have iron shutters; and when the doors and windows are closed no air can possibly enter the buildings. There is no lining to the iron, either in the way of ceiling or walls. There is no flooring, except mother earth.

In the girls' house (may leaven pardon me for so describing) that kennel there are three rough bunks in which a sailor would flatly refuse to sleep. There are no sheets seemingly, no blankets; no pictures on the walls; not enough chairs to seat half a dozen people; no veranda, so that the heat or the cold or the rain must beat directly on to the walls of the buildings. In rainy weather, which, fortunately does not come very often, either the place must be sealed or the floor becomes a puddle.

If rain and heat come together the interior of these buildings must be like the Black Hole of Calcutta. The hottest period on record in Alice Springs was one of eight consecutive days, during which the temperature was over 100 degrees every day.

There is no need to fear the cold. When the girls go to bed (and my measurements are generous), they have each exactly a space of six feet by two to accommodate them from end to end of the building, and even mountain air at 4000 feet cannot overcome the self generated heat of such packing. The boys are just as well off in that aspect.

NO BATHING.

There is no water supply at the school; the children themselves carry whatever water is needed over 100 yards from the police bungalow, and across the main road. There is one small lavatory, no bathroom, except such as is improvised with a tub there is not enough table accommodation to let these beings—many of them as say, as white as anyone else, and often supported at the private expense of their white fathers—sit down and have their meals like civilised beings; if there were there would be no chairs or forms for most of them to sit on. The cooking accommodation consists of a sort of sentry box affair with an ordinary stove in it, which would send the ordinary housewife on strike if she were asked to cook for a family of ten on it. The cooking hutch is up to the winds that blow; the cook and superintendent is an old black gin.

"HALF A WOMAN."

"Now, this is all bad enough but what follows is worse. The supervision which the Government provides for this institution is half a white woman. Not a whole one, mind you. Half of her is supposed to devote her time to teaching the white school. The other half to clothing, managing supervising morals, putting to bed, getting up, washing, and dressing of 50 children. who are sometimes not all in health, and who range from infancy to the age of motherhood. (Some of the girls in this place already have babies of their own.)

She must supervise the hewing of wood, the drawing of water, the teaching, the cooking—every detail of their lives. She has no toys to amuse them; the scantiest library from which to teach them; no forms for them to sit on—not even a blade of grass on which they may play games, for the "bungalow" faces a dusty public road, and the ground about it is worn bare by the incessant patter of small feet.

For assistance she had a gin or two gins. I forget which it is, but if the language of the one whom I met was an earnest of the obscenity of the other, I should hope that the second does not exist. Even assuming there were two good gins—they would be of little use. However, they seem to be two bad ones, of evil reputation among the community, and yet for three parts of the time they are in full charge of the youngsters—including the nights. At night the doors cannot be locked. Inevitable trouble results. Residents of Central Australia a hundred miles from Alice Springs told me that the place was a moral cesspit, and if the stories which they related were only an eighth true (I cannot say myself) they would make the whole community recoil with horror if they could be repeated.

All I do know is that the report of this condition of affairs was prevalent right into Darwin, and for support there is the remark of the Acting Chief Protector of Aborigines, written as far back as 1921, which says:—

"MOST UNSATISFACTORY."

"This bungalow has been, and is, very unsatisfactory, being in immediate touch with the public and near an hotel. Girls leave the premises and visit men at night, returning to the bungalow before daylight. Some boys and girls have been hired under agreement to reputable persons in South Australia, and their behaviour has been satisfactory."

How calm it all sounds, this report of four years ago. Girls—mark you, white as anyone else—girls who can learn to read and write and spell; girls who can be taught to be clean and save money; girls who retain sufficient affection for their teacher and only friend to write to her two years after they have gone into service at Adelaide—leave the premises and visit men at night, returning before daylight!

And the good Protector finds it "most unsatisfactory." And passing Ministers write platitudes in the visiting book—carefully-conceived platitudes, which show how anxious they are to avoid responsibility of knowledge. And nobody does anything about it.

And one woman is slaving her life out for those girls, and actually succeeding. more or less, in keeping them clean, and teaching them to read and spell by dint of working 15 hours a day. And her own experience—one half-caste 17 year old girl is her housekeeper, and has her little cottage as charming a picture of cleanliness as you could see anywhere—and that of Mrs MacDonald, who manages the half-caste school at Darwin, prove that it is worth while.

THE MURDER OF SOULS.

The Darwin children are a picture of cleanly health. The girls wear pretty dresses. The boys are neatly clad. The broad-veranda bungalow is well furnished. There is sewing or housework going on in the sewing room. No white school would have cause to be ashamed of the atmosphere of the manners or accomplishments of the inmates. They look a happy and a useful family. Many of them wear boots and stockings.

At Alice Springs bungalow the appearance of everybody and everything convicts the Home and Territories Department of the progressive destruction of 50 young promising human lives and souls.

I indict the department on that charge.

```
                              Aboriginal Compound
                                Darwin, 21st June, 1927.


The
  Chief Protector of Aboriginals

     D A R W I N.


Sir,

        I beg to draw your attention to the conditions at the
Half-caste Home Darwin, which come under my supervision.

        The building occupied by the inmates of the Home has a
floor space of 2275 square feet, namely: 35 ft X 65 ft. this
space comprises three rooms with a 9 ft. 6 in. verandah all
around. A bathroom, a pantry and a linen room are partitioned
off within the verandah. This building is considerably over-
crowded as the number of occupants at present is 44 including
very small motherless children. The building is not only too
small but it is very much out of repair insomuch that the floor
is rotten in many places, the lattice work broken in many parts,
no plunge bath, no lining on the bathroom floor, the shower is
out of order and the locks on most of the doors are not secure.

        In the Kitchen which adjoins the building, the stove is
unfit for use and the sink together with the table has collaps-
ed causing all slops to fall on the floor and drain through to
the ground beneath the building where it mingles with that from
the laundry tubs and bathroom which, likewise, have no downpipes
to carry such drainage to the proper source, in fact very little
if any, ever reaches the concrete drain which is provided for the
purpose. The inmates of the Home have all to bath at least once
a day and all crockery in use have to be washed up three times a
day as well as the 44 changes of clothing besides water used for
scrubbing the whole of the Home once a day.

        The whole building and kitchen require painting for they
present a very dirty appearance in spite of all efforts to keep
them clean.

        The number of inmates in the home is too large for the
pan accommodation in the lavatories.

        In view of the fact that there are over 30 Half-castes
yet to come into the Home in the near future the building is
far too small and I submit the accommodation is unsuitable.


                          Yours Faithfully,

                            Harold S. Giles

                          Supt: Compound.
```

OPPOSITE PAGE
Reports of poor living conditions at the Bungalow received wide publicity in the southern newspapers. *(Australian Archives)*

Those who ran the homes often sought improvements, usually with little success. Here the Superintendent of the Kahlin Compound complains to the Chief Protector of Aboriginals about conditions in the 'half-caste' home in 1927. *(Australian Archives)*

Children eating breakfast at the Bungalow, Alice Springs, 1923 *(Australian Archives)*

7. *Live white, think white*

We were taken away at nine years old and brainwashed towards living the white society instead of living the old Aborigine way. We were brought in to forget that sort of thing.
George Bray

In the homes the part-descent children would learn white ways. They were encouraged to forget their Aboriginal background and to 'live white, think white.'

Contact with Aboriginal culture was restricted. Once the 'half-caste' home was moved outside of Kahlin Compound in Darwin, the children were rarely allowed contact with their full-descent relatives living on the other side of the fence. At the Bungalow, the children were forbidden to speak their own languages.

Formal schooling was seen as the road to civilisation for these children. One-teacher schools were set up early at the Bungalow and at Kahlin Compound, where the children learnt 'stories of famous men or great explorers' and 'the extent of the British Empire.' The standard of schooling was poor, and in both homes the problems were the same: too few teachers, too many students and poor facilities. It was not until the 1930s that more teachers were employed and the standard of education improved.

Alice Springs,
Half-caste Institution,
13ᵗʰ Feb. 1940.

District Officer,
    Alice Springs.
                Dear Sir,
                    The following
material is required at the above
school.

1. 1 chair.
2. 2 glass tumblers.
3. 10 domestic arts manuals.
4. 1 Map of World.
5. 24 small brushes for applying
    paste.
6. 1 tin jade green paint (Quick Enamel)
7. 9 pictures. — coloured and
    framed with narrow antique
    frames. The following are
    suggested.
        (1) Dutch flower scene on side of
            canal
        (2) Sunset at Venice
        (3) Sailing ship at sea in
            moonlight.
        (4) The Vigil.
        (5) A Hunting Scene.
        (6) Landing at Sydney Cove.
        (7) Pictures of elves and fairies
        (8)
        (9)
8. 1 tin black board paint.
9. 1 pair large cutting-out scissors
    for dress-making.

Letter from the school teacher at the Bungalow, Old Telegraph Station, Alice Springs, requesting supplies for the school, 1940
(Australian Archives)

School fife band at the Bungalow, Old Telegraph Station, Alice Springs, c.1939
(Boehm Collection, courtesy Conservation Commission of the Northern Territory)

School inspection report by
V. L. Lampe, Inspector of
Schools, for Kahlin 'Half-caste'
School, Darwin, 1936
(Australian Archives)

Most children were baptised
into one of the Christian
denominations while in the
homes. This memorandum sets
out the government's policy on
religious instruction at the
Bungalow in 1934.
(Australian Archives)

DEPARTMENT OF THE INTERIOR.

CEH ——————

No. 33/1096

MEMORANDUM:

Religious Instruction - Half-caste Institution,
Alice Springs.
——————————

        The position in regard to the Religious
Instruction of children at the Half-caste Home, Alice Springs,
is set out very clearly by Dr. McCann in his report of the
24th October,1934.

2.   On the 10th November,1932, the Minister approved
of the adoption of a suggestion made by the Chief Protector
of Aboriginals "that the mothers should be permitted to
nominate the denominations into which they desire their
children to be baptized and that in the case of orphans of
12 years of age and over a personal expression of preference
should be accepted."

3.   According to Dr. McCann, 74 children are definitely
baptized in the Church of England, 21 in the Roman Catholic
Church and 29 are unbaptized.

4.   Once a child is baptized in a particular Church,
that Church should be responsible for the further religious
instruction of the child. Any attempt at proselytism should be
stopped immediately, because it will only lead to trouble and
will result in confusing the child's mind.

5.   It is doubtful whether any satisfactory solution
of the trouble will be forthcoming from a Conference of the
heads of the various denominations interested.   The Bishop
of Carpentaria, who saw me in Darwin in regard to this matter,
is quite definite that the Church of England is responsible
for the religious welfare of the children baptized in that
Church. It is to be presumed that the Roman Catholic Church
will adopt the same attitude.

6.   It is recommended -

  (a) that the decision given by the Minister on the
     10th November,1932, stand; and

  (b) that Religious Instruction to the children who
     have already been baptized be given by the
     Ministers of the Churches in which they have been
     baptized.

7.   It is competent for the Rev. Mr. Griffiths to
concentrate his efforts on the 29 children who have not been
baptized.

APPROVED

JPaterson

Minister ... Interior

13/11/34.

Girls dancing to fife band at the
Bungalow, Old Telegraph
Station, Alice Springs, c.1939
*(Boehm Collection, courtesy
Conservation Commission of the
Northern Territory)*

SCHOOL INSPECTION.

Kahlin Half-Caste School - Darwin.

September 7th., 16th., 21st., 1936.

          Number on Roll 3 Boys + 40 Girls Total 43.
Present at Inspection. 3 "   36 "   " 39.

Staff. Head Teacher - Mrs. H.W. Carruth (Appointed May, 1929).

I.   **RECORDS.** Neatly and correctly kept.

II. **GOVERNMENT.** Discipline apparently presents no difficulties. The fact that school is held on a verandah only ten feet wide makes effective supervision very difficult. Some of the children are inclined to trust to their own keen eyesight and their neighbours' work instead of working for themselves. The children are orderly, but the spirit of eagerness and earnest endeavour appears to be lacking, though this may be due to the diffidence of the children in the presence of a comparative stranger.

III. **ORGANISATION.** Unsatisfactory. Despite written instructions in the form of an amended curriculum the Head Teacher has attempted too much and accomplished very little. The programme of lessons was up-to-date but set out too vaguely. In Arithmetic the entry for some Grades for several consecutive months was "Sums from the Cards". This is far too indefinite. The programme of work should show definitely just what has been done.

IV. **METHODS.** In some cases these were not such as to tend to develop the intelligence of the children. Greater use must be made of charts and sketch maps in the teaching of History and Geography. Oral testing showed that the children have evidently been used to prompting, and without prompting show up very poorly.

V.   **PROFICIENCY AND PROGRESS OF CHILDREN.**
    1. **Reading.** Fairly correct. Expression is weak, and the comprehension is poor. Tonelessness in reading is a characteristic of coloured children, but efforts should be put forth to induce a brighter and more expressive tone.

    2. **Recitation.** The pieces were not known either collectively or individually, The children have apparently relied too much on prompting. Expression was lacking.

    3. **Spelling.** Despite some individual weaknesses this was a satisfactory subject.

    4. **Dictation.** This was weaker than the Spelling.

    5. **Writing.** A satisfactory subject. Pupils should use the copy books set for their respective Grades. Errors in the formation of individual letters need explanation on the blackboard.

    6. **Grammar.** A weak subject.

    7. **Composition.** Ideas were very limited, especially on a new subject. The reproduction of previous compositions was better.

    8. **Mathematics.** In written Arithmetic the mechanical work in Grade IV was very good, elsewhere it was moderate. Anything in the nature of a problem was badly done. Simple problems should be given often, both in written and oral work. The mental Arithmetic was weak; tables were not well-known, whilst notation

1.

A Year and a Bit at the Bungalow

Maise Chettle (nee Robb) – teacher at the Bungalow, Alice Springs, 1935–36

In the Gazette of the South Australian Education Department late in 1934 appeared a notice calling for applications for the position of teacher at the Home for 'Half-caste' Children recently established at the Old Telegraph Station near Alice Springs. I was chosen to fill the position.

When I arrived at the Bungalow at the beginning of the 1935 school year the Superintendent and the Matron, Mr and Mrs Jones, came out to meet me. They took me to the schoolroom, the battery room of the old telegraph days. It was an elongated, whitewashed stone building with seven windows on one long side and one on each end. There was a wide veran-dah, flywired and fitted with roll-up canvas blinds, similar to all the houses in the town at that time.

The students were already seated in an assortment of desks; the legs of some of the tiny children did not reach the floor, but that did not seem to trouble them. They all looked squeaky clean with hair combed and plas-tered down; the boys in freshly laundered khaki shirts and shorts, and the girls in blue striped cotton frocks, all with wide welcoming grins and sparkling eyes. This was the

same every morning but by the end of each day in that hot weather, with red dust inches deep on the ground, none of us looked so very clean.

There were eighty-two of them of various ages and sizes, some well into their teens. Their hair and complexion varied too from very fair to dusky brown. I was told that the names on the roll were not always those of their real fathers. Sometimes it was the name of the station or district where they were born or their mother's name, but one did not go into those matters. We struggled with the arithmetic exercises and the copy books, the spelling and grammar, the latter by far the most difficult. The most popular lessons were singing and drawing; not the set tonic solfa scales and the draw-ing of objects in perspective, but singing along with Matron Jones' wind-up gramophone records of popular country and western and minstrel songs. Now and again I would allow 'free choice' for drawing, with wonderful results. They drew their every-day experiences with gusto – the animals, wild and herd; all types of vehicles, even aeroplanes.

It was no easy task to teach eighty-two children at various stages of ability. Halfway through the year an assistant

teacher was appointed and the verandah was turned into a second classroom for the two younger grades. With the can-vas blinds rolled up this was a fairly cool, breezy place in the hot weather; even in the cool season the days were sunny, so it was never really cold.

After school, household chores were done – carrying in wood for the kitchen stove and bringing in the washing – but there was plenty of time for games. When there was a safe depth of water in the waterhole, swimming was first choice for all. Sometimes the boys went fishing up the creek with sticks, string and safety pins; they played crick-et with mulga boughs cut roughly into bats; the girls played a kind of hockey with sticks fashioned likewise and old tennis balls. After seeing these games one visitor from Melbourne sent a tea-chest full of bright pictures, boiled sweets, cricket bats and balls, but, sadly for the girls, no hockey sticks!

There was little sickness among the children except for the drastic trachoma, which affected the eyes and was much aggravated by the mica in the red sandy soil. Both the Jones' children suffered from it badly. Dr Riley came regularly and did his best to ease it.

The end of the year brought three special occasions for the children, all in conjunction with the students of the town school. There was sports day, where the Bungalow children easily out-ran and out-jumped the town children. Then there was a bountiful picnic lunch supplied by the tradespeople of the town and managed by the parents' committee of the town school. Finally there was the Christmas party, complete with Father Christmas, a tree, and presents for all. The Bungalow children gave a con-cert, based largely on our singing lessons, with appropriate actions and costume. The town people lit up the concert area with their car headlamps. It was an hilarious success with coloured cordials and iced cakes for supper.

My year and a bit at the Bungalow remains a happy memory; a bright spot, I am told, in its history. At a reunion there in 1994, arranged by a daughter of one of the girls, I had the pleasure, at the age of eighty-eight, of meeting some of my former scholars with their grandchildren.

Children at the Kahlin Compound beside the fence dividing the compound from the 'half-caste' home, 1930s
(E. H. Wilson, courtesy AIATSIS pictorial collection)

School room at the Bungalow, Old Telegraph Station, Alice Springs, 1936
(Rennison-Menz Collection, courtesy Conservation Commission of the Northern Territory)

8. Worktime, playtime

**We wasn't bored in any way
whatsoever. We made our own fun.**
George Bray

Apart from several hours of schooling each weekday, all children did work around the homes. The girls made clothes, and helped with washing, cleaning, baking bread and caring for the small children. The boys helped tend the garden, carry wood and look after the goats. Many older girls who had left school worked as domestic servants for white families during the day and returned to the homes at night.

But the children still found time to play. In the early years, little recreation was organised in the homes, so they relied on their own ideas. In later years at the Bungalow the children played organised sports such as hockey, cricket and rounders. Trips to the pictures were a special treat. Christmas was 'the best time of year' when the children received presents of small toys and sweets.

Hockey game at the Bungalow,
Old Telegraph Station, Alice
Springs, 1935
*(Chettle-Robb Collection, courtesy
Conservation Commission of the
Northern Territory (CCNT))*

Boys looking after the goats at
the Bungalow, Old Telegraph
Station, Alice Springs, c.1939
*(Boehm Collection, courtesy
CCNT)*

Domestic arts class at the
Bungalow, Old Telegraph
Station, Alice Springs, c.1939
*(Boehm Collection, courtesy
CCNT)*

Identification discs, known as 'dog tags', were issued to Aboriginals living in Kahlin Compound in 1932. They were probably also worn by girls who lived at the home but worked outside during the day.
(Australian Archives)

OPPOSITE PAGE
The average daily routine for Mrs Freeman, Matron of the Bungalow, Old Telegraph Station, Alice Springs, 1933
(Australian Archives)

DARWIN ABORIGINES NOW LABELLED

Issue Of Identity Discs Amuses Them: "All Same Dog"

DARWIN, Monday.—Aborigines summoned to submit themselves for compulsory medical examination are being supplied with identity discs.

"All same dog," they say, although it is not compulsory for them to wear the medals round the neck. They can be kept "alonga pocket."

The aborigines are being officially advised that presentation of the medals will be necessary when they are seeking admission to picture shows or making withdrawals from trust accounts deposited on their behalf by employers. The medals will obviate the possibility of a native of the same name drawing the earnings of another boy.

The medal is of bronze, with a raised edge. On one side there is a large embossed crown over a number. A red tape suspensory is attached to enable the medal to be worn round the hat or neck. The natives are highly amused.

The chief protector (Dr. Cook) stated today that one aborigine was highly indignant at not receiving a medal "all same other boys."

The aborigines are clever at making colored bead necklets and armlets. These will replace the red tape before very long, that is, unless the medals are bartered in the meantime as a final stake of gambling.

DEPARTMENT OF HOME AFFAIRS.

No. 32/1067

MEMORANDUM:

METAL DISCS FOR ABORIGINALS.

The Administrator of the Northern Territory asks that a quotation by obtained from the Defence Department for the supply of brass discs containing identification numbers for issue to aboriginals in town districts employed under licence and agreement.

He states that the Chief Protector of Aboriginals desires these discs in order to secure greater control over the employment of aboriginals and to check the employees entering and leaving the Compound.

It will be necessary to obtain further particulars from the Administrator in regard to the size, number, wording etc. of the discs, but before any action is taken in the matter, it seems desirable that the Minister should indicate whether he approves of the suggestion.

All aboriginals employed in the town of Darwin must be in the Compound between the hours of 7 p.m. and 6 a.m., unless special permission to remain on the premises of the employer has been given by a Protector.

Although the issue of identification discs might be objected to by some of the Societies interested in the welfare of aboriginals on the ground that the practice is degrading to the aboriginal, it is felt that the Chief Protector would not recommend the adoption of this course unless he had good grounds for doing so in the interests of the aboriginals themselves.

Personally I see no objection to the practice. There must be times when it is extremely difficult for the Chief Protector or the Superintendent of the Compound to make an accurate check on the inmates of the Compound in order to ensure that none of them is roaming about the town at night and indulging in practices detrimental to their welfare, such as drinking of liquor, opium smoking, etc.

10. 2. 1932.

Half-Caste Institution:- Alice Springs:-

Example of an average days work routine for the Matron.

6.A.M. Rising Bell. Open Girls Dormitory .
Attend to Hospital "In" patients. (if any)

7. " Inspect kitchen and see to breakfast and breadmaking.
See that Laundry girls are proceeding with the daily washing.

7.30 " Supervise the serving of breakfast with Supt.
" Hospital patients breakfast.

8.30 " General attendance at hospital for minor complaints, attend to
patients,(if any)and cleanliness of hospital.

9.30 " See that Kitchen girls are preparing the midday meal and baking
bread, pantry and dining room girls have cleaned up, and general
supervision and instruction in the dormitories, as to cleanliness
making beds etc. See that the daily baths are being proceeded with
with also that all children are clean and tidy for IO.A.M. school.

IO. " See children into school with Supt.
Attend to the preparation of midday meal.
See that the Washing girls have finished ,and give daily instruct
ion in mending and ironing.
(clothing changed daily.)

IO.30
or II." School or Hospital work to attend to.

I2.Noon. Supervise dinner, for inmates and patients(if any)

I. P.M.See that dining room girls are proceeding with washing up and
cleaning.

2. " Sewing classes for the girls, cutting out and dressmaking, knitting
and fancy work:- and/or assisting with the school.to 4.I5.p.m.

5. See to the preparation of supper.

7.I5. Attend evening prayers with Supt.

7.30. See that all small children are put to bed, and lock back doors
of Dormitories.

8. See that the girls are setting bread, and when necessary instruct
them. (all girls are taught to make bread.)

8.30. Attend hospital if necessary:- a final look round at the small
children and girls.

9. Lock all doors, and"lights out"

    many small duties are performed during the day which,it is impossible
to enumerate:- it must be distinctly understood that although a large
amount of the above work, maybe classified as supervision, it is far
more, being "constant" instruction which is most essential for the
satisfactory training of these people.

                        Matron,
                    Half-Caste Institution.

List of Christmas gifts ordered for children at the Bungalow, Old Telegraph Station, Alice Springs, 1934
(Australian Archives)

Playing cricket at the Bungalow, 1935
(Chettle-Robb Collection, courtesy Conservation Commission of the Northern Territory)

Christmas Tree List.

Half-Caste Institution
Alice Springs
21-11-34.

Allowance £ 20-0-0

Soap Cakes, Palm-olive or Lux	2 doz.	@ 4/6.		9 - 0
Needle - Cases.	8	@ 1/6.		12 - 0
Ladies Stockings, Lisle, beige Ladies	13 pairs	@ 3/-		1 - 19 - 0
Enamel Brooches assor.	22	@ 1/-		1 - 2 - 0
Hair - Clasps.	21	@ 1/-		1 - 1 - 0
Beads - Boxes.	18	@ 1/-		18 - 0
Necklaces. assor.	8	@ 1/6.		12 - 0
Colored Balls.	6	@ 1/-		6 - 0
Dolls.	24	@ 1/6.		1 - 16 - 0
Pocket Knives	7	@ 1/6.		10 - 6
Gyroscope Tops	12	@ 9		9 - 0
Marbles	24 dozen	@ 2 for doz.		4 - 0
Mouth Organs	5	@ 1/6.		7 - 6
Dice Games.	7	@ 1/3.		8 - 9
Hard Rubber Balls	17	@ 1/-		17 - 0
Mechanical Toys. Assor.	22	@ 1/6		1 - 13 - 0
Pull-along Trucks.	9	@ 1/6		13 - 6
Trumpets	9	@ 6		4 - 6
Rattles.	6	@ 1/-		6 - 0
			£	14 - 8 - 9

Freight about £ 2-0-0				2 - 0 - 0
Grams - Records for childrens Gramophone.				
8 Regal Records @ 2/6. -				1 - 0 - 0
1 Football				1 - 2 - 6
2 games Table Tennis @ 3/11				7 - 10
2 games Draughts @ 1/-				2 - 0
1 Cricket Comp. Ball @ 2/6				2 - 6
1 dozen Balloons. @ 2				2 - 0
			£	19 - 5 - 7

Balance in boiled lollies.

9. *Out in the wicked world*

You had nobody else but that group that was in the Home with us. I can still remember the heartaches when I left those kids.
Daisy Ruddick on leaving Kahlin

Most children had to leave the homes at around age fourteen. The boys would go out to work on pastoral stations, often working long hours for no pay. Most girls found work as domestic servants for white families, either in the Territory or down south. Some children ran away, and a few returned home to their families.

By 1941, the government had decided that care of part-descent children should be handed over to the church missions. The children were to be divided by religion: those baptised as Roman Catholics would be sent to Melville Island, Methodists to Croker Island, and Church of England children to other locations.

Kahlin 'Half-caste' Home was closed in 1939 and the children moved to the new Bagot Reserve. When the reserve was taken over by the military at the start of the Second World War, the part-descent children were sent to the church missions.

The Bungalow was closed in 1942, by which time most of its children had been sent to missions on Croker and Melville islands. When the islands were evacuated during the Second World War the children were sent to the southern states, where they lived in mission care for several years, far from their kin and their country. Some were never to return home.

/6

HO/644

HO/o/4576

ADMINISTRATOR,

DARWIN, N.T.

20th May, 1941.

The Secretary,
Department of the Interior,
CANBERRA.   A.C.T.

TRANSFER OF HALF-CASTE CHILDREN.

With reference to this subject, I desire to inform you
that the transfer of half-caste children from Pine Creek to
Mission Stations is proceeding very satisfactorily.

Thirty-eight children are now en route to the Methodist
Mission at Goulburn Island.   A lugger (the "South Seaman") has
been hired and is being escorted by the "Larrakia".   All possible
precautions in regard to safety have been taken.

The transfer of other personnel from Pine Creek to
Delissaville is now in progress.

The first lot of children will move up from the Alice
Springs Half-Caste Home for transfer to various Missions towards
the end of this month.

The Roman Catholic Half-Caste Homes at Garden Point, on
Melville Island, have been completed and are ready to receive
their proportion.   The Roman Catholic authorities have applied
for a Mission Lease of 133 square miles on Melville Island. and
this is now being prepared.

A Depot has also been established in Apsley Straits
which will be utilised as a control station for pearling luggers
and a rationing point for indigent and aged aboriginals.

Refractory aboriginals will be transferred to Melville
Island or to Delissaville, as the case may be.

I am very pleased with the work and organisation
displayed by Mr. White, the Secretary of the Native Affairs
Branch, and his staff.

HO/o/ 0816
7551
5206.

Seen

H. S. Foll.

30/5/41

(C.L.A. Abbott)
ADMINISTRATOR

8/7

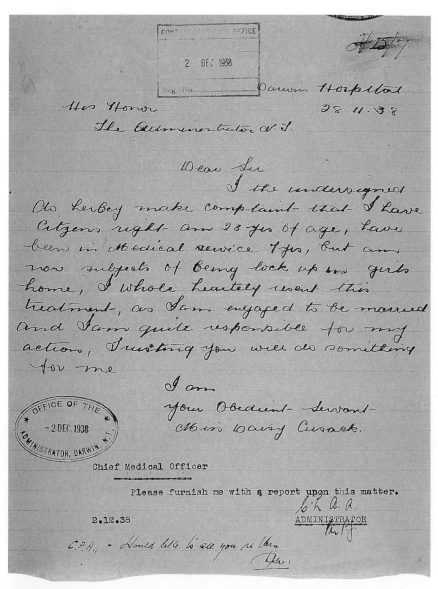

OPPOSITE PAGE
Letter from the Northern
Territory Administrator,
C. L. A. Abbott, regarding the
transfer of children from the
government homes to church
missions, 1941
(Australian Archives)

Letter from Daisy Cusack (now
Ruddick), seeking permission
to leave the Kahlin 'Half-caste'
Home, Darwin, 1938
(Australian Archives)

Daisy Cusack, second from left,
and friends, Darwin, c.1930s
(Courtesy Daisy Ruddick)

In 1934 the Minister for the Interior had a plan to find new homes in the southern states for children from Kahlin and the Bungalow. Following the appearance of this article in the Melbourne *Herald,* a Melbourne woman wrote to the minister offering to take one of the girls. Although children from the homes were occasionally adopted out to white families by informal arrangement, the minister's initial plan was never developed into a formal policy.
(Australian Archives)

Homes Are Sought For These Children

A GROUP OF TINY HALF-CASTE AND QUADROON CHILDREN at the Darwin half-caste home. The Minister for the Interior (Mr Perkins) recently appealed to charitable organisations in Melbourne and Sydney to find homes for the children and rescue them from becoming outcasts.

I like the little girl in Centre of group, but if taken by anyone else, any of the others would do, as long as they are strong

Methodist girls at the Bungalow, Old Telegraph Station, Alice Springs, before leaving for Croker Island, c. 1941
(Boehm Collection, Conservation Commission of the Northern Territory)

OPPOSITE PAGE
Letter from William Bray, George Bray's father, protesting against the evacuation of his children from the Bungalow, 1941
(Australian Archives)

Protector   Alice Springs
    Aboriginals.   Central Australia (N.T.)
                                April   1947

Dear Sir.

— I myself, and my wife, both half castes we
understand, do not want any of our
children removed, out of this Central Australia
their country.

— It would not be fair to us, the loss of
them. Also not fair to them the loss of
their parents, causing crying and fretting.

— We parents, born Arltunga goldfields.
Children also, except one, he being the eldest,
Norman. He born Deep Well, part of the
east-west running James Range.

— As we were all born here in Central
Australia, we don't know any other
parts, and don't want to.

— Will you please place this
Protest, as we do not understand
~~as we do not understand~~ any forcible
removal, of any of us, from this Central
Australia, our birth-right country.
            Yours truly W. Bray

(W. BRAY = HIS SIGNATURE)

20   The Australian Women's Weekly   December 29, 1945

Half-castes will have own colony in North

Young evacuees spent happy schooldays with white children

By MERTON WOODS

Seventy half-caste aboriginal children, innocent victims of fate and war, are soon to start an adventure designed to bring them pride and happiness.

They will be the first occupants of a colony for half-caste waifs established by the Methodist Mission on Crocker Island, north of Darwin.

THE missioners plan to educate and instruct as many half-caste children as possible until they can fill an accepted place in Australia's community life.

The 70 half-caste children who will be the first party sent to Crocker Island are now living at Otford, picturesque South Coast hamlet 32 miles from Sydney.

They were moved to Otford in June, 1942, when the threat of Japanese invasion caused their evacuation from Crocker Island.

At Otford they have lived in a spacious country home owned by the Methodist Mission.

They have all gone to school in Otford's two-room schoolhouse, learning to read, write, sing, and paint, alongside the white children of Otford's residents.

For three years the white children have accepted their new classmates without question, have vied with them at lessons, and romped with them at playtime.

This year 55 half-castes and 20 white children went to Otford School.

Six of the half-caste girls attended Wollongong High School, one boy went to Woonona School, and eight older girls are in domestic service in Sydney homes.

Before being succored by the Methodist Mission, many of the children were despised and unwanted waifs.

One, Marjorie, a nine-year-old of Javanese-aboriginal blood, was rescued four years ago from a sordid opium den in Darwin.

Marjorie has normal powers of speech, but because in the opium den she was threatened with violence if she spoke or cried, she has made herself "dumb."

She does not speak to the other children or to her schoolteachers, Mr. C. W. Greentree and Miss Marcia Smith, or to Methodist Missioners Miss J. K. March and Miss Margaret Sommerville, who run the Otford Mission House.

But she laughs and plays with the other children, making signs to let them know what she needs. They attach no significance to Marjorie's "dumbness."

When the children first came to Otford, many knew no other names than those the missioners had bestowed on them.

Some of the girls changed their Mission Christian names to those of their favorite film stars.

One child who bears a striking resemblance to Claudette Colbert insists on being called "Claudette."

Until they began to mingle with the white children at Otford, the half-castes did not know the meaning of birthdays.

But when they learned that on a certain day each year a white classmate received gifts and strangely became a year older, they decided to get into the birthday business, too.

So 70 random dates, judiciously spaced by Miss March, were chosen by the children as their birthdays.

High intelligence

MR. GREENTREE, who has taught the half-castes for two and a half years, considers their intelligence is as high as that of any white children he has taught in his 20 years as a teacher.

He has mastered the extraordinary shyness which dominates the relations of these children with white people.

The children's shyness has been gradually overcome, and they now reveal their knowledge individually. But they prefer written tests, in which they co-operate enthusiastically.

All of them show very high musical and artistic ability.

Mr. Greentree cites the six half-caste girls attending Wollongong Domestic Science School as typical examples of the half-castes' intelligence.

Wollongong Domestic Science School wished to put these girls in a special class, but the Mission authorities suggested they attend classes with white pupils.

Since then the half-caste girls have topped their classes in art, physiology, and English.

Miss J. K. March, head missioner at Otford, worked for 15 years at a mission at Rabaul (New Britain). She and Miss Sommerville evacuated the children from Crocker Island.

They will return with the children. Miss March said: "Because Australia has such a small population it cannot afford to discard anyone as outcasts.

"We intend to make the children who will pass through our hands at Crocker Island living examples of the good that can be extracted from aboriginal half-castes.

"We want half-caste boys and girls reared on Crocker Island to marry and live on their own farms on the island.

"We plan to give the girls a sense of self-respect, self-confidence, and responsibility, so that, either on their own account or with the help of the Mission, they can manage restaurants, cake shops, or dressmaking shops in Darwin."

HAPPY SMILES from some of the half-caste children evacuated from the Northern Territory three years ago. They are being cared for at a Methodist Mission Home at Otford, N.S.W.

WHITE CHILDREN shared desks with their dusky schoolmates at Otford Public School. Mr. C. W. Greentree is the teacher.

Many of the children from Kahlin or the Bungalow who had been sent to Croker Island in 1941 were evacuated to Otford in New South Wales when the Japanese entered World War II. This article is about their return to Croker Island at the end of the War.
(Australian Archives)

10. Mission homes

Missionary didn't let us go, you see. She bin learn us to speak, like white man way. Know about a white god story, teaching us to do longa white man way.
Hagar Roberts

Kahlin and the Bungalow were not the only Aboriginal children's homes in the Northern Territory. Most church mission stations included a home, sometimes for part-descent children but often for all Aboriginal children. There have been more than a dozen mission homes in the Territory.

Life for the mission children was similar to life in the government homes. Girls learned the Bible and a little reading and writing, sewing and cleaning. The boys worked in the garden, looked after the animals, or trained for stockwork. Most were not allowed to see their mothers and fathers even when they lived on the same mission station. They wore European clothes and were forbidden to use their own language. Some children loved the missionaries as if they were their parents, others spent much of their time trying to escape.

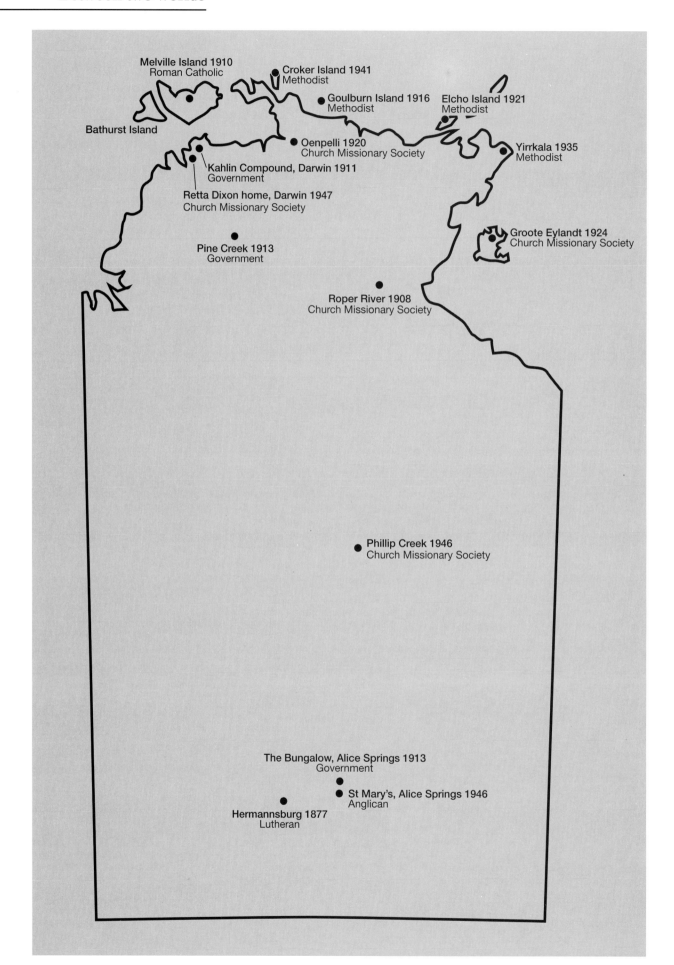

Melville Island 1910
Roman Catholic

Croker Island 1941
Methodist

Goulburn Island 1916
Methodist

Elcho Island 1921
Methodist

Bathurst Island

Oenpelli 1920
Church Missionary Society

Yirrkala 1935
Methodist

Kahlin Compound, Darwin 1911
Government

Retta Dixon home, Darwin 1947
Church Missionary Society

Groote Eylandt 1924
Church Missionary Society

Pine Creek 1913
Government

Roper River 1908
Church Missionary Society

Phillip Creek 1946
Church Missionary Society

The Bungalow, Alice Springs 1913
Government

St Mary's, Alice Springs 1946
Anglican

Hermannsburg 1877
Lutheran

Major Aboriginal children's institutions and missions in the Northern Territory with dates of establishment

Oenpelli Mission, 1928
(Australian Archives)

School at Goulburn Island Mission, 1928
(Australian Archives)

Mission School, Bathurst Island
(Australian Archives)

Children at Hermannsburg
Mission, early 1900s
(Australian Archives)

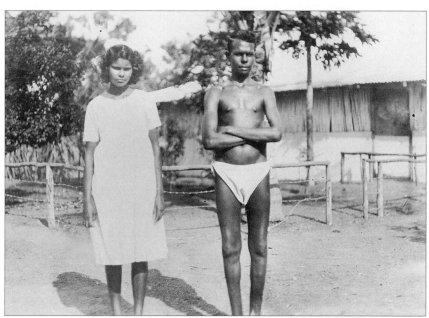

This photograph appeared in
the Bleakley report of 1928.
The original caption reads:
'Half-caste boy and girl,
Goulburn Island Mission. Since
sent to Southern College for
vocational training.'
(Australian Archives)

Children at Hermannsburg
Mission, early 1900s
(National Library of Australia)

11. *Changing times*

No child shall be removed except where the child is neglected or in need of medical care.
Director of Native Affairs, 1952

By the early 1950s, the wisdom of separating part-descent children from their families was being questioned. Some patrol officers, distressed at heart-rending removal scenes, refused to take children away. The 'half-caste' institutions in Darwin and Alice Springs which had been closed during the war did not re-open.

In 1953 a new Welfare Ordinance replaced previous laws about child removal. Aboriginal children would no longer be removed from their families simply because they were of part descent. Children of any race could be removed if they were judged to be 'destitute' or 'neglected'. Through the eyes of white officials, many part-descent children seemed to fit this description. They continued to be removed from their families, but under different laws.

In 1957 there were over sixty part-descent children in institutional care in the Northern Territory. In an effort to segregate them from full-descent Aboriginals many were placed in church-run 'island homes' on Croker and Melville islands. Some remained in the Retta Dixon Home in Darwin, while others were sent to South Australian institutions or were adopted.

Finally the government accepted that separation from their kinfolk did not help children to gain a place in white society. The 'island home' policy was abandoned in the 1960s, though it was not until 1980 that the last Darwin homes were closed.

Retta Dixon Home, Darwin, c.1961 *(Australian Archives)*

Woman bathing a child at the Retta Dixon Home during the 1950s
(National Library of Australia)

Retta Dixon Home, Darwin, c.1958 *(Australian Archives)*

(The photographs on this page were taken by the Australian News and Information Bureau and used by the Commonwealth government as publicity shots to advertise Australia overseas.)

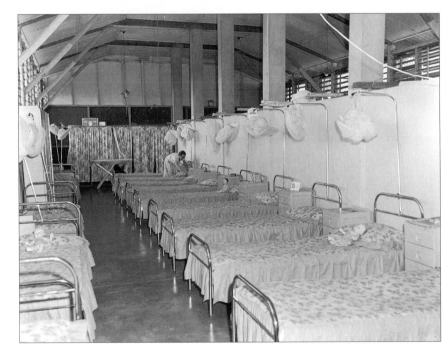

OPPOSITE PAGE
Comments like those of Patrol Officer Evans prompted the government to reconsider its policy on the removal of part-descent children in the early 1950s *(Australian Archives)*

KAR.

4th January, 1950.

<u>HIS HONOUR THE ADMINISTRATOR.</u>

<u>NATIVE WELFARE.</u>

In Patrol Officer Evans' report, dated 23rd December, 1949, on his patrol to the Wave Hill - Timber Creek Areas, the following passages occur:-

"<u>Comment.</u>

The removal of the children from Wave Hill by MacRobertson Miller aircraft was accompanied by distressing scenes the like of which I wish never to experience again. The engines of the 'plane are not stopped at Wave Hill and the noise combined with the strangeness of an aircraft only accentuated the grief and fear of the children, resulting in near-hysteria in two of them. I am quite convinced that news of my action at Wave Hill preceded me to the other stations, resulting in the children being taken away prior to my arrival.

I endeavoured to assuage the grief of the mothers by taking photographs of each of the children prior to their departure and these have been distributed among them. Also a dress length each was given the five mothers. Gifts of sweets to the children helped to break down a lot of their fear and I feel that removal by vehicle would have been effected without any fuss.

<u>Recommendations.</u>

(1.) I accordingly recommend that only in extreme cases is removal of part-aborigines effected by aircraft.

(2.) That if possible the children be left with their mothers until they are at least six years of age. At this age they are beginning to free themselves of maternal ties and are at the same time at a suitable age to begin their education. The alternative to this is that they be removed at the age of twelve months which, for obvious reasons, would involve complications beyond the scope of a Patrol Officer.

Which brings me to another point which I ask be given consideration - the appointment of an itinerant female welfare worker to assist native mothers on cattle stations and to help in the gentler removal of part-aboriginal children. In my opinion a native mother would be far readier to hand over her offspring to the care of a white woman than to the mercies of a male."

This refers to what I am assured by the Acting Director of Native Affairs is the practice of removing half-caste children from their aboriginal mothers to Darwin or some other suitable centre for care and education.

I cannot imagine any practice which is more likely to involve the Government in criticism for violation of the present day conception of "human rights". Apart from that aspect of the matter, I go further and say that superficially, at least, it is difficult to imagine any practice which is more likely to outrage the feelings of the average observer.

sometimes accepted and the mother invariably returns to her country satisfied.

In the northern part of the Territory, such children are sent to the Garden Point Mission Station, the Croker Island Mission Station, or the Retta Dixon Home, Darwin. In the southern portion, the institution used for this purpose is St. Mary's Hostel.

The total number of partly coloured boys and girls in these institutions at present is:

Boys - 163   Girls - 194

I am satisfied that the practice of moving partly coloured girls and boys from native camps and nomadic conditions to institutions of the kind mentioned is in accordance with the Government's policy of assimilation, and is in the best interests of the white and black communities and, subject to certain safeguards enumerated below, should be approved by the Minister.

I recommend, therefore, that future policy be based on the following principles:-

(a)   Partly coloured children found in aboriginal camps or a similar environment may be removed, if the Director of Native Affairs thinks it necessary in the interests of the children, to a suitable institution.

Approved

(b)   No such child shall be removed without the written approval of the Director of Native Affairs.

Approved

(c)   The officer removing the child shall hold such powers delegated to him by the Director as may be necessary to effect the removal lawfully.

Approved.

(d)   No child under the age of 4 years shall be removed except where the child is neglected or in need of medical care or the mother expressly requests the removal.

No age limit need be stated. The younger the child is at the time of removal the better for the child. Please amend comma, as shown, to read to the beginning clear c

(e)   No child shall be removed, except where it is neglected or is in need of medical care or the mother expressly requests its removal, until the Director is satisfied that a painstaking attempt has been made to explain to the mother the advantages to be gained by the removal of the child.

(f)   The mother is to be permitted to accompany her child, if she so desire, to Darwin and Alice Springs, to satisfy herself that the child will be well cared for.

Approved

(g)   Aircraft shall not be used for the removal of a child except where no other method of transport is available.

Approved

(h)   All children shall be medically examined without undue delay upon removal at Darwin and Alice Springs.

Approved

(i)   A report shall be made by the Director to the Administrator immediately after the 30th June in each year showing the names and ages of children removed during the year, the circumstances of removal in each case, the name of the institution to which

Approved. These reports are to be confidential for official use only c

"Cruel policy" on native babies

ADELAIDE, Tues.—The Federal Government is cruel in ordering that half-caste babies must be taken from their mothers at the age of three months, says Dr. Charles Duguid.

Taking babies from the mothers was the most hated task of every patrol officer, said Dr. Duguid.

He was addressing the annual meeting of the Aborigines' Advancement League after his election as president last night.

Dr. Duguid said the policy of the Federal Government to separate half-castes and full-bloods was wrong.

The half-caste children were sent either to Melville Island or Croker Island, until they were 18. They were then free to come to the mainland.

"A more humane policy must be devised," said Dr. Duguid.

"The Federal Government has decided to educate all full-blooded aborigines, even on the stations. Its policy is to absorb the aborigines into the white race.

"In view of this, surely it would be better to let half-caste babies grow up with their mothers in their own country."

By the 1950s the policy of removal was becoming more openly criticised, as shown in this article from the Melbourne *Herald,* 1951
(Australian Archives)

Retta Dixon Home on Bagot Aboriginal Reserve, Darwin, c.1958
(Australian Archives)

Article from the Melbourne
Age regarding the adoption of
some Croker Island girls by a
Melbourne family, 1957
(Australian Archives)

From Croker Mission to Brighton Mansion

TWO YOUNG ABORI-GINAL children and a 19-year-old girl have suddenly been moved from the austere sur-roundings of a Method-ist mission on Croker Island to life in a man-sion in East Brighton.

They are Christine (4½) and Faye (2) Deutsher and Dozi Simpson, 19, who have been adopted by Mr. and Mrs. W. A. Deut-sher, of Milliara Grove, East Brighton

Mr. Deutsher saw the three girls when he was touring the Northern Territory last Septem-ber and asked the mis-sion authorities if he could adopt them.

Mr. Deutsher said last night that the way to solve the native prob-lem was to bring them into the homes of white people so that they could be thoroughly acclimatised.

Mr. Deutsher's fine home is now theirs—it includes a television set, which fascinates the youngsters.

"It is a strange new world for them and a tremendous step in their lives," Mr. Deut-sher said.

Mr. Deutsher is the proprietor of W. A. Deutsher Pty. Ltd., pro-duction engineers, Brighton.

The picture shows Mr and Mrs. Deutsher and their daughter Lorraine, with the three aboriginal girls around the piano at home last night.

12. **Same story, different places**

The story of my family is not unique. It is echoed thousands of times over the length and breadth of Australia.
Sally Morgan

Almost every state had its own Act of Parliament by which Aboriginal children could be separated from their families. The exception was Tasmania, where the government had denied for many years that there were still Aboriginal people living in the state. Most state laws referred to all Aboriginal children, whether of part or full descent.

No-one knows how many children were taken away across Australia, but in New South Wales alone the number was probably greater than 10,000.

Children removed from their families were usually declared to be wards of the state. They may have been sent to a church or a state Aboriginal children's institution, placed with a foster family, or adopted. The new parents were almost invariably non-Aboriginal.

Some of the children were taught to be so ashamed of their Aboriginal descent that they pretended all their lives that they were really white or of some other nationality. Some children never even knew that they were Aboriginal. They would never know that they had other names, other relatives and other homes, in places they had never heard of.

St Francis Boys Home,
Semaphore, South Australia,
c.1951
(Australian Archives)

Kinchela Boys Home, New
South Wales, c.1959
(Australian Archives)

Children at Colebrook, South Australia, c.1930
(United Aborigines Mission, AIATSIS pictorial collection)

Kinchela Boys Home, New South Wales, c.1959
(Australian Archives)

61

Boys dormitory class,
Cherbourg, Queensland, c.1930
*(E. Brainwood, AIATSIS
pictorial collection)*

Girls dormitory, Cherbourg,
Queensland, c.1930
*(J. Bond, AIATSIS pictorial
collection)*

Croker Island Mission, 1956
(National Library of Australia)
(This photograph was taken by
the Australian News and
Information Bureau and used
by the Commonwealth
government as a publicity shot
to advertise Australia overseas.)

13. *Coming home*

Then we went back to Wattie Creek. When the car pulled in, my two brothers were there. They hadn't seen me for sixty years, but they knew. They said 'Hello my sister.'
Daisy Ruddick

Did the children who were taken away ever come back home? Some children who had not lost contact with their families returned home as soon as they left the institutions. Many lived most of their lives apart from their families and did not find their way back home until years later. Others are still looking for their people today.

With the help of the Aboriginal organisation Link-Up (see Appendix), Aboriginals across Australia are making their way home again. Link-Up helps people removed as children to find their families and helps families find their children that were taken away. Link-Up workers accompany those who were removed when they first meet their family again. They also help them cope with any problems they have dealing with the experience of removal, or of coming home after many years of separation.

Daisy Ruddick (centre) with some of her family at Lajamanu, c. 1986. Daisy was taken away to the Kahlin 'Half-caste' Home at the age of six, and did not find her family again until sixty years later. *(Courtesy of Daisy Ruddick)*

Hilda Muir

When you went out to work you went out to work for your living. I don't remember that I was thinking about wanting to go back and try and find my mother, or see her, or see the country. I'm not bitter for what I got out of it: civilisation, education. But I always just regret that I didn't go back earlier to see my mum. That's the only thing that I'm just sad about today, not seeing my mum. But that's the only regret I have now, I never seen my mother. If only I could've seen her face. If only we went a bit earlier, you know, if my daughter got married a bit earlier. When we went back and I wanted to see my mother, they said, 'Oh, she died a couple of years.' I just missed out. People says she was a wonderful lady.

Emily Liddle

A lot of kids didn't even know where they come from. I don't think they knew, they were too small when they come into town. We was all right because we knew where our mother lived, and it was all right for us, but we used to feel so sorry for the little ones that come there.

Alec Kruger

I often thought to myself now, why did they take me away? Like after I grew up and that, I said, I often thought to myself, now why did they take me away. Like it's not to educate me or anything, they took me away to be a slave for the European station owners.

Bungalow Days
Herbie Laughton

As the twilight's deep shadows surround me
Here alone by the old waterhole
And my thoughts are of mates all around me
In the days of the old Bungalow.

I remember the good times together
As a lad all so carefree and gay
Our contentment forever and ever
Will remain to the end of my days.

I can picture the old home so clearly
As it was many years long ago
And I'll cherish those memories so dearly
Of the days at the old Bungalow.

So let me dream once again by the river
Where as a lad I was carefree and gay
For the old place will bring back sweet memories
Of the days at the old Bungalow.

Happy days are the saddest of memories
Childhood memories bring teardrops to flow
While I dream here beneath the old gum tree
I remember the old Bungalow.

I can picture the old home so clearly
As it was many years long ago
And I'll cherish those memories so dearly
Of the days at the old Bungalow.

Poster produced by Link-Up (Queensland) Aboriginal Corporation, 1993

George Bray

No-one knew who their parents were – only the parents of course – and they never seen their parents until – some of them were grown up before they went back and seen their parents.

14. *Tr*ue stories

There's a lot of pain having fingers, legs broken. But it takes a lot longer to repair spirits, minds. That takes a whole lifetime.
Margaret Brusnahan

Photograph by Wayne Miles

Hilda Muir was born at Borroloola in 1920. Her mother was Managoora Mara (Polly), a Yanua woman. Hilda's Aboriginal name is Jaman. She was taken away at the age of eight to the Kahlin 'Half-caste' Home in Darwin. She stayed there until she was fourteen, when she began nursing and lived at the Darwin Hospital. Hilda did not return to Borroloola until 1973, where she discovered that her mother had only recently died. She now lives in Darwin and returns often to Borroloola to visit her people. She has ten children, thirty-five grandchildren and nineteen great-grandchildren.

OPPOSITE PAGE
Emily Liddle, third from right, and family today
(Courtesy of Ponch Hawkes)

Hilda as a young woman, standing at left
(Courtesy of Hilda Muir)

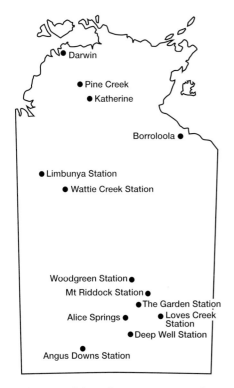

Some of the places mentioned in the stories.

Photograph by Richard Williams

Emily Liddle was born Emily Perkins at Deep Well Station in 1919. Both her mother Alice Grant and her father Bert Perkins were Arrernte people of part descent. At the age of nine Emily was taken away to the Bungalow, where her mother would visit her every Sunday. She left when she was about fifteen to do domestic work for an Alice Springs family, and later moved to Angus Downs Station. She now lives in Alice Springs and has eleven children, twenty-one grandchildren and eight great-grandchildren.

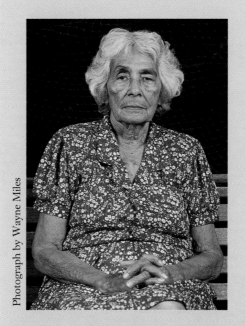

Photograph by Wayne Miles

Daisy Ruddick was born Daisy Cusack on Limbunyah Station in 1916. Her mother was Lizzie, a Gurindji woman, and her father was John Cusack, an Irishman. Daisy's Aboriginal name was Kumachi; later she was called Nola. She was taken away to the Kahlin 'Half-caste' Home at the age of six and stayed there until she was thirteen, when she left to work for a Darwin family. Daisy went in search of her family in 1983, and met her brothers for the first time in sixty years. She now lives in Darwin and keeps in contact with her people at Wattie Creek. She has three daughters, seven grandchildren and two great-grandchildren.

Photograph by Richard Williams

George Bray was born at Stone Well on Mt Riddock Station in 1927. Both his mother Mary and his father William were Arrernte people of part descent. At the age of nine George was taken away and placed in the Bungalow with his brother and three sisters. He lived there until he was thirteen, when he went out to work at The Garden Station. George never lost contact with his parents, who sometimes visited him at the Bungalow. He now lives in Alice Springs and has ten children, and many grandchildren and great-grandchildren.

George Bray as a child, front row, left. Emily Liddle is in the middle of the back row.
(Courtesy of George Bray)

Photograph by Richard Williams

Alec Kruger was born in Katherine in 1924. His mother was Polly Wurrumbaru, a Jawoyn woman, and his father was Frank Kruger, a white man. Alec's Aboriginal name was Bumbolili. He was taken away at the age of three and placed in the Kahlin 'Half-caste' Home in Darwin. Along with the other boys from the home, Alec was sent to Pine Creek in 1931, then to the Bungalow in Alice Springs in 1933. He left at the age of eleven, when he went to work at Loves Creek Station. In 1942 he joined the army. Alec did not meet his mother again until more than twenty years after he was taken away. He now lives in Alice Springs and has six children and twelve grandchildren.

Alec Kruger as a soldier during the Second World War, front row, left
(Courtesy of Alec Kruger)

Photograph by Richard Williams

Herbie Laughton was born at Alice Springs in 1927. His mother was Amy Laughton, an Arrernte woman of part descent, and his father was Simon Reef, a Russian. Herbie was placed in the Bungalow with his brother and mother in 1930. His mother left the home in search of work after she married Mick Laughton, but continued to visit her children there once a year. Herbie left the Bungalow at the age of eleven to work at Woodgreen Station and some years later returned to Alice Springs to live with his mother. He now lives in Alice Springs, and has six children and twelve grandchildren.

Herbie Laughton as a young boy, reclining in middle of front row. Emily Liddle is in the middle of the second back row.
(Courtesy of George Bray)

Appendix

Carol Kendall   *Link-Up*

Generation after generation of Aboriginal children all over Australia have been removed from their families and communities and placed in institutions, adopted or fostered out. Link-Up works to assist these people to find their way home to their natural families, their Aboriginal communities and culture.

Link-Up's aim is to empower Aboriginal people to take control and make decisions that affect their lives. For many this may be the first opportunity they have to do so and it can be very frightening. Link-Up assists in working through the effects of removal and separation to prepare people for a successful reunion, and helps them to come home by accompanying them as they meet their families for the first time.

Support group meetings in most states and territories address the issues of grief, loss and trauma suffered through the experience of being removed. And as most Aboriginal communities across the country have had large numbers of their children taken, the grief and loss felt by the whole community is also addressed.

The process of researching and locating information on Aboriginal families can be very difficult. Many Aboriginal people's births, marriages or deaths have not been formally registered, and the only source of information lies in the memories of some of the older people, which can be very distressing for them. It can involve remembering a time that may have been a painful emotional experience both for them and the community, particularly if their own children had been removed.

Many rural Aboriginal people lived and worked on cattle or sheep stations, so a useful source of information is the station log books. One woman who was unsure of her birth date knew that her parents had worked on a sheep station in outback New South Wales. She visited the property and asked if they still had the old log books. The owners were very obliging and gave her access to them. Here she found among the daily entries recording the births of lambs and calves a reference to a daughter born to her parents.

In another case a non-Aboriginal historian was visiting a small Aboriginal community when a very frail woman approached her and asked, 'Do you know where they took my daughter?' She related how her four-year-old daughter had been taken away in a plane to go to school with the assurance that the child would be returned. This happened forty years ago. The historian knew of Link-Up and told the woman she would pass the request on to us.

Around that time a younger woman contacted Link-Up, looking for her natural family. She told us she had been taken from them and put on a plane and that she did not know her family's name or where they came from. Native Welfare had placed her in a Christian home for Aboriginal children on an island off the Northern Territory coast. She lived there until she was fifteen and the children there became like a family to each other.

Some of the staff at the home were kind, but many were not. She was taught that Aboriginal people were bad and that she would be better off associating with non-Aboriginal people. She was never told anything about her natural family or where she had been taken from. Later she was fostered by a non-Aboriginal family, who lived thousands of miles away in another state. Once again she was removed from her 'family' and placed in a totally different environment.

She had a very happy home life with her foster family, but she felt and looked different. There were feelings within her that she couldn't understand. She loved her foster family, but she needed to find her own identity and her family.

Link-Up tried to get access to government records and to files held by the Christian home, and after years of searching finally discovered where the woman came from and her family name. When she was reunited with her family, she made a visit with her mother to the airstrip where they had been separated more than forty years before.

The journey home is, however, just the beginning and the larger part of Link-Up's work lies in counselling after the reunion. Re-establishing links with family and community doesn't happen automatically; there are many differences to overcome: the person who was removed may have a different name, may not speak the same language, and may know nothing of their own culture and history. The process of healing and recovery can sometimes take many years. Link-Up provides assistance for as long as it is useful, and it is offered to all family members including the adoptive or foster family.

There is a saying which sums up the Link-Up philosophy: 'You have to know where you come from to know where you're going.' Link-Up emphasises pride in Aboriginality, and the necessity of both coming to terms with the past and taking courage to step into the future.

Link-Up contact groups

NEW SOUTH WALES/ACT
Link-Up (NSW) Aboriginal
Corporation
5 Wallis Street
LAWSON 2783
(PO Box 93 LAWSON 2783)
Tel: (047) 59 1911

NORTHERN TERRITORY
Karu: Aboriginal and Islander
Child Care Agency
PO Box 40639
CASUARINA 0811
Tel: (08) 8922 7171

Central Australian Aboriginal
Child Care Agency
9 Kemp Street
ALICE SPRINGS 0870
(PO Box 2438 ALICE SPRINGS
0871)
Tel: (08) 8953 4895

QUEENSLAND
Link-Up (Qld) Aboriginal
Corporation
8 Gillingham Street
BURANDA 4102
(PO Box 1128 COORPAROO
4151)
Tel: (07) 3891 2554

SOUTH AUSTRALIA
Department of Family and
Community Services
Family Information Service
Aboriginal Link-Up
11 Hindmarsh Square
ADELAIDE 5000
(Box 39 Rundle Mall 5000)
Tel: (08) 8226 6823

TASMANIA
Tasmanian Aboriginal Children's
Centre
7a Emily Road
WEST MOONAH 7009
Tel: (03) 6272 7099

VICTORIA
Victorian Aboriginal Child Care
Agency
34 Wurruk Avenue
PRESTON 3072
Tel: (03) 9471 1855

WESTERN AUSTRALIA
Yorganop Aboriginal Child Care
Agency
Unit 44a Piccadilly Square
Cnr Nash & Short Streets
PERTH 6000
Tel: (09) 227 9022

Bibliography

Tony Austin, *I Can Picture the Old Home So Clearly: the Commonwealth and 'Half-caste' Youth in the Northern Territory 1911–1939,* Aboriginal Studies Press, Canberra, 1993

J. W. Bleakley, *The Aborigines of Australia,* Brisbane, 1961

G. C. Bolton, 'Black and White after 1897' in C. T. Stannage (ed.), *A New History of Western Australia,* University of Western Australia Press, Nedlands, 1981

Commonwealth of Australia, *Aboriginal Welfare: Initial Conference of Commonwealth and State Aboriginal Authorities, held at Canberra, 21 to 23 April 1937,* Government Printer, Canberra, 1937

Commonwealth of Australia, Parliamentary Papers 1913, vol. III, Preliminary report on the Aboriginals of the Northern Territory by Professor W. Baldwin Spencer

Barbara Cummings, *Take This Child . . . from Kahlin Compound to the Retta Dixon Children's Home,* Aboriginal Studies Press, Canberra, 1990

Anna Haebisch, *For Their Own Good: Aborigines and Government in the South West of Western Australia 1900–1940,* University of Western Australia Press, Nedlands, 1988

John Harris, *One Blood: 200 Years of Aboriginal Encounter with Christianity – A Story of Hope,* Albatross, Sutherland, 1990

Andrew Markus, *Governing Savages,* Allen & Unwin, Sydney, 1990

Peter Read, *Charles Perkins; A Biography,* Viking, Melbourne, 1990

C. D. Rowley, *Outcasts in White Australia,* Penguin, Ringwood, 1973

Tim Rowse, 'Assimilation and After' in Ann Curthoys, A. W. Martin and Tim Rowse (eds), *Australians from 1939,* Fairfax, Syme and Weldon Associates, Sydney, 1987

Archival sources

Australian Archives (ACT): CRS A1; 1930/1542; Prof. Sir Baldwin Spencer. Visit to NT re: Natives at Alice Springs (1921–1924); contains W. B. Spencer's Report on the Half-castes and Aboriginals of the Southern Division of the Northern Territory, with special reference to the Bungalow at Stuart and the Hermannsburg Mission Station, 10 September 1923

Australian Archives (ACT): CRS A1; 1929/5189; G. W. Burns Visit Cent Aust June 1929; contains The Aboriginals and Half-castes of Central Australia and North Australia: Report by J. W. Bleakley, Chief Protector of Aboriginals, Queensland, 1928

Australian Archives (ACT): CRS A1; 1927/2982; Alice Springs Bungalow Central Australia [File No. 1] (1914–1929)

Australian Archives (ACT): CRS A659; 1939/1/996; Half-caste Home, Alice Springs, NT [File No. 2] (1928–1939)

Australian Archives (ACT): CRS A659; 1939/1/15580; Half-caste Home, Darwin (1923–1940)

Australian Archives (NT): CRS F1; 1938/366; Kahlin Compound, Aboriginal Compound and Half-caste Home (1933–1938)

Australian Archives (NT): CRS F1; 1937/30 Half-caste Home, Alice Springs (1932–1937)

Australian Archives (NT): CRS F1; 1942/70A; Half-caste Institution (Alice Springs) to November 1938 (1938)

Australian Archives (NT): CRS F1; 1942/70B; Alice Springs Half-caste Institution from December 1938 to December 1942 (1938–1942)

Northern Territory Archives Service Oral History Collection: Interview with George Bray, NTRS 1726, TS 659, 1991

Northern Territory Archives Service Oral History Collection: Interview with Emily Liddle, NTRS 1726, TS 660, 1991

Northern Territory Archives Service Oral History Collection: Interview with Hilda Muir, NTRS 219, TP 913, 1993

Institute for Aboriginal Development: recorded interview with Alec Kruger, 1990

Individual archival sources

Chapter 1: Life on the fringes

p. 2   *'Half-caste' man and woman with their child;* source: AA(ACT): CRS A1; 1930/1542; photo 1
Children at No. 3 Bore, Northern Territory, c.1920; source: Ferguson Collection, National Library of Australia
Elcho Island, Northern Territory, 1937; source: AA(ACT): CRS M438; photo 37

p. 3   *Alexandria Station, Northern Territory, 1917;* source: National Library of Australia, Pictorial Collection, NL27231
Mother and child, Northern Territory, c.1928; source: AA(ACT): CRS A263; [7b(3)]

p. 4   *Aboriginal camp on Lamaru Beach, Darwin, 1913;* source: Parliamentary Papers, 1913, Volume 3, Preliminary Report on the Aboriginals of the Northern Territory by Baldwin Spencer, pp 264–80
Buffalo hunters, Alligator River, Northern Territory, c.1928; source: AA(ACT): CRS A263; [35b]
Bathurst Island, Northern Territory, c.1928; source: AA(ACT): CRS A263; [27b]
Children at Alexandria Station, Northern Territory, c.1917; source: National Library of Australia, NL27229

Chapter 2: Black, white and shades of grey

p. 6   *Baldwin Spencer's report of 1913 reflected scientific views of the day about the Aboriginal race;* source: Parliamentary Papers, 1913, Volume 3, Preliminary Report on the Aboriginals of the Northern Territory by Baldwin Spencer, pp 264–80
Spencer caricature; source: Low, David, 1915, *Caricatures by Low: Collected from the Sydney 'Bulletin' and Other Sources,* Tyrell's, Sydney.

p. 7   *Cross cartoon, Smith's Weekly, 1920, 1922; Glover cartoon, The Bulletin, 1927; soap advertisement, 1920s;* source: Swain, David, 1988, *200 In the Shade, An historical selection of cartoons about Aborigines,* William Collins, Sydney

p. 8   Levy-Bruhl, Lucien, *How Natives Think,* George Allen & Unwin Ltd, London; source: National Library of Australia
Porteus, Stanley D., *The Psychology of A Primitive People. A Study of the Australian Aborigine,* Edward Arnold & Co, London; source: National Library of Australia
Stoddard, Lothrop, 1922, *The Rising Tide of Color Against White Supremacy,* Chapman and Hall Ltd, London; source: National Library of Australia
Whither Away? A Study of Race Psychology and the Factors Leading to Australia's National Decline, 1934, Angus & Robertson Ltd, Sydney; source: National Library of Australia
This 1920s newspaper article summarises popular white views about Aboriginals of part descent; source: AA(ACT): CRS A1; 1927/2982 (Adelaide *Advertiser,* 8 Nov 1924)

Chapter 3: The road to a civilised life

p. 10   *Children at the Bungalow, 1920s;* source: Spencer Collection, Museum of Victoria Council

pp. 10–11   *Early government planning for the establishment of an institution for part-descent children, 1911;* source: AA(ACT): CRS A1; 1911/18824 (dated 23 Oct 1911)

p. 11   *General View of Kahlin Aboriginal Compound, Darwin, 1915;* source: Museum of Victoria, Ethnohistory collection

pp. 12–13   *Extracts from the* Aboriginals Ordinance 1911 *which authorised the government's removal of Aboriginal children of part descent;* source: AA(ACT): CRS A1; 1912/2937

p. 14   *The Bungalow, Alice Springs, 1921;* source: AA(ACT): CRS A3; 1922/2805 (Plate VII)
Children at Kahlin Compound, Darwin, 1915; source: Museum of Victoria, Ethnohistory collection
Children at Kahlin 'Half-caste' Home, Darwin, 1920s; source: Daisy Ruddick

Chapter 4: The last goodbye

p. 16   *'Half-caste' mother and child;* source: AA(ACT): CRS A263; [7b(4)]
Group of prisoners, witnesses, interpreters and part-descent children being taken by police to Alice Springs in the 1930s. The children were bound for the Bungalow; source: Northern Territory Archives Service, NTRS 234, CP 496/4; McKinnon Collection

p. 17   *Northern Territory police officers, 1938;* source: AA(ACT): CRS M107; photo 86
'In 1932 I had the job of taking this half-caste child from its parents and taking her to Alice Springs Government Half-caste Institution. Such jobs were most unpleasant and even dangerous.'; source: Northern Territory Archives Service, NTRS 234, CP 495/1; McKinnon Collection

pp. 18–19   *The Borroloola Police Journal of 1928 records Hilda Muir's removal to Kahlin 'Half-caste' Home in Darwin;* source: Northern Territory Archives Service, F268 NT Police Journal – Borroloola, 14/11/1927–6/6/1931

Chapter 5: Breed him white

p. 21   *Kahlin 'Half-caste' Home, Darwin, 1928;* source: AA(ACT): CRS A263; [25a]
Two girls at the Bungalow, 1920s; source: AA(ACT): CRS A1; 1930/1542; photo 5
J.W. Bleakley, Queensland's Chief Protector of Aboriginals and Dr Cecil Cook, the Northern Territory's Chief Protector, 1928; source: AA(ACT): CRS A263; [68a]

pp. 22–23   *J.W. Bleakley's 1928 report in which he recommended that 'half-castes' continue to be removed from Aboriginal camps for placement in institutions;* source: AA(ACT): CRS A1; 1929/5189

p. 24   *The Bungalow, Alice Springs, 1928;* source: AA(ACT): CRS A263; [6a]
Letter from Dr Cecil Cook regarding his plan to eventually eliminate the part-descent population by 'breeding

out the colour', 1933; source: AA(ACT): CRS
A659/1; 1940/1/408 (dated 7 Feb 1933)

p. 25   *This newspaper article reflects white fears of the 1930s
about the growing part-descent population in the north;*
source: AA(ACT): CRS A659/1; 1939/1/996
(Sydney *Sun*, 2 April 1933)

Chapter 6: Life in the homes

p. 27   *This photograph was taken by Dr W.D. Walker who
visited the Bungalow at Alice Springs in 1928;* source:
AA(ACT): CRS A1; 1928/10743; photo 49
*Meal time at the Kahlin 'Half-caste' Home, Darwin,
1930s;* source: AIATSIS pictorial collection, E.H.
Wilson, N3636.71
Meal time at the Bungalow, 1928; source: AA(ACT):
CRS A1; 1928/10743; photo 44

p. 28   *This weekly diet list for the Kahlin 'Half-caste' Home
was the official ideal. Few former residents recall regularly eating roast beef or fried steak;* source: AA(NT):
CRS F1; 1938/366 (dated Oct 1938)

p. 29   *Article from the Sydney* Bulletin *condemning poor condi-
tions at the Bungalow, Jay Creek, 1929;* source:
AA(ACT): CRS A659/1; 1939/1/996 (dated 14
Aug 1929)

p. 30   *Reports of poor living conditions at the Bungalow
received wide publicity in the southern newspapers;*
source: AA(ACT): CRS A1; 1927/2982 (Brisbane
Daily Mail, 13 Nov 1924)

p. 31   *Those who ran the Homes often sought improvements,
usually with little success. Here the Superintendent of the
Kahlin Compound complains to the Chief Protector of
Aborigines about conditions in the 'half-caste' home in
1927;* source: AA(ACT): CRS A1; 1937/15140[g]
(dated 21 June 1927)
*Children eating breakfast at the Bungalow, Alice
Springs, 1923;* source: AA(ACT): CRS A1;
1930/1542; photo 8

Chapter 7: Live white, think white

p. 33   *Letter from the school teacher at the Bungalow, Old
Telegraph Station, Alice Springs, requesting supplies for
the school, 1940;* source: AA(NT): F1; 1942/91
(dated 13 Feb 1940)
*School fife band at the Bungalow, Old Telegraph
Station, Alice Springs, c.1939;* source: Boehm
Collection, Conservation Commission of the
Northern Territory, NTHP 804

p. 34   *Most children were baptised into one of the Christian
denominations while in the homes. This memorandum
sets out the government's policy on religious instruction at
the Bungalow in 1934;* source: AA(ACT): A1;
1933/4488 (dated 13 Nov 1934)
*Girls dancing to fife band at the Bungalow, Old
Telegraph Station, Alice Springs, c.1939;* source:
Boehm Collection, Conservation Commission of
the Northern Territory, NTHP 810

p. 35   *School inspection report by V.L. Lampe, Inspector of
Schools, for Kahlin 'Half-caste' School, Darwin, 1936;*
source: AA(ACT): A1; 1936/9959 (dated Sept 7th,
16th, 21st 1936)

p. 37   *Children at the Kahlin Compound beside the fence
dividing the compound from the 'half-caste' home, 1930s;*
source: E.H. Wilson, AIATSIS pictorial collection,
N3636.73
*School room at the Bungalow, Old Telegraph Station,
Alice Springs, 1936;* source: Rennison-Menz
Collection, Conservation Commission of the
Northern Territory, CCNT 2610

Chapter 8: Worktime, playtime

p. 39   *Hockey game at the Bungalow, Old Telegraph Station,
Alice Springs, 1935;* source: Chettle-Robb Collection,
Conservation Commission of the Northern
Territory, ASTS–00707
*Boys looking after the goats at the Bungalow, Old
Telegraph Station, Alice Springs, c.1939;* source:
Boehm Collection, Conservation Commission of
the Northern Territory, NTHP 820
*Domestic arts class at the Bungalow, Old Telegraph
Station, Alice Springs, c.1939;* source: Boehm
Collection, Conservation Commission of the
Northern Territory, NTHP 815

p. 40   *Identification discs, known as 'dog tags', were issued to
Aboriginals living in Kahlin Compound in 1932. They
were probably also worn by girls who lived at the home
but worked outside during the day;* source: AA(ACT):
CRS A1; 1934/4166 (article: Melbourne *Herald*, 12
Sept 1932)
*Memorandum explaining the purpose of the identifica-
tion discs, 1932;* source: AA(ACT): CRS A1;
1934/4166 (dated 10 Feb 1932)

p. 41   *The average daily routine for Mrs Freeman, Matron of
the Bungalow, Old Telegraph Station, Alice Springs,
1933;* source: AA(ACT): CRS A1; 1935/643 (dated
17 Feb 1933)

p. 42   *List of Christmas gifts ordered for children at the
Bungalow, Old Telegraph Station, Alice Springs, 1934;*
source: AA(NT): CRS F1; 1942/70(A) (dated 21
Nov 1934)
Playing cricket at the Bungalow, 1935; source:
Chettle-Robb Collection, Conservation Commission
of the Northern Territory, ASTS–00736

Chapter 9: Out in the wicked world

p. 44   *Letter from the Northern Territory Administrator, C. L.
A. Abbott, regarding the transfer of children from the
government homes to church missions, 1941;* source:
AA(ACT): CRS A431/1; 51/1399 (dated 20 May
1941)

p. 45   *Letter from Daisy Cusack (now Ruddick), seeking permission to leave the Kahlin 'Half-caste' Home, Darwin, 1938;*
source: AA(NT): CRS F984; Cusack (dated 28 Nov
1938)
Daisy Cusack and friends, Darwin, c.1930s; source:
Daisy Ruddick

p. 46   *In 1934 the Minister for the Interior had a plan to find
new homes in the southern states for children from Kahlin
and the Bungalow;* source: AA(ACT): CRS A1;
1934/6800 (dated 20 July 1934)
Methodist girls at the Bungalow, Old Telegraph Station,